ZANESVILLE
STONEWARE
COMPANY

Identification & Value Guide

Jon Rans —///— Glenn Ralston —///— Nate Russell

COLLECTOR BOOKS

A Division of Schroeder Publishing Co., Inc.

Cover design: Beth Summers
Book design: Melissa J. Reed

COLLECTOR BOOKS
P.O. Box 3009
Paducah, Kentucky 42002-3009
www.collectorbooks.com

Searching for a publisher?

We are always looking for people knowledgeable within their fields. If you feel that there is a real need for a book on your collectible subject and have a large comprehensive collection, contact Collector Books.

Contents

Introduction 4
Acknowledgments 4
Background 6
    Ohio Encaustic Tile Company 7
    E. G. Bowen and Company 12
The Zanesville Stoneware Company 13
    History 13
    Production 26
    Garden Ware 29
    Marks and Identification 36
Glaze and Shape Identification 41
    Matte Green 42
    Matte Lavender 60
    Matte Rose 62
    Matte Blue 67
    Gloss Black 70
    Gloss White 73
    Gloss Yellow .74
    Seacreast Green 76
    Gloss Aqua 79
    Gloss Rose 81
    Gloss Blue 82
    Rubble Ware 87
    Omar Ware 91
    Hand Thrown Ware 93
    Ebonello 96
    Vulcan 97
    Neptune 99
    Zasko 104
    Verdantone .110
    Vorosa 112
    Montrose 113
    Brown and Tan Overflow 114
    Forest Green Overflow 120
Variety Glazes, Shapes, and Novelties 123
    Country Fare 145
Catalog Pages .147
Bibliography 270
About the Authors 271

Introduction

Every collector of American art pottery has pieces in their collection that are unidentified and unmarked. I hope this book sheds some light on one of those potteries that often present a mystery. At first glance the qualities of Zanesville Stoneware pottery are often overlooked, but these simple forms and harmonious glazes warrant closer inspection. Zanesville pieces' visual subtlety and depth and texture are seldom seen in items produced by their contemporary production potteries.

Acknowledgments

A word of thanks to all who made this book a reality by sharing their time, information, and collections: Bud and Andy Linn of the Zanesville Stoneware Company for the use of their remaining catalogs, photographs, and family history; Michael Sims, who researched the Ohio Encaustic Tile Company and supplied photographs of tile selections; Glenn Ralston and Nate Russell, long-time collectors who brought their expertise and talent to the book; and Pat Ralston for her photos and interviews from 1989.

A special thanks is given to the collectors of Zanesville Stoneware who allowed their lives to be interrupted and pottery pieces to be photographed for this project: Adam Sack and Jen Szekely, Hand Thrown Ware and Omar Ware; Keith Redman and Paul Stanley, Old Pot Shop ware; Ted Ackley, Zanesville Stoneware collection; and Don Escovar, plant workers photo. Their expertise, patience, and contributions are greatly appreciated.

Hugh and Jana Ward, thanks for the photographs of your collections, aid in research, and taking the time to help. Thanks to Raymond A. Burns, who at the last hour provided photographs and information. Also, thanks to the New Orleans Conservation Guild, Inc., for their help.

Thanks to the staff of the Muskingum County Library for their help in locating published articles, and the staff of Collector Books for publishing assistance and believing in my project. Last but not least, thanks to my wife Rita for her aid and encouragement throughout this project. Thank you all.

Jon Rans

Steamship *Valley Gem* carried goods throughout the Muskingum and Licking riverways.

Canals played a vital role in early trade and commerce.

5

Background

Due to its natural vast clay deposits, Ohio has been home to many potteries, some famous and others almost unknown. Located in east central Ohio, Zanesville is in the heart of this clay-rich region.

Circa 1890s. Zanesville city promotion ad.

The first pottery to produce ware in the Zanesville area was started by Samuel Sullivan. With his initial success, "Clay City" became home to many local potters.

The nearby village of Putnam excelled in the making of stoneware. Stoneware articles were so important to the local economy as a source of trade and wealth that stoneware was referred to as "Putnam currency." Putnam was annexed by Zanesville in 1872.

Early uses of stoneware were clearly utilitarian. Storage crocks and jugs along with other useful items were needed by every family. The tonnage of clay products as brick, tile, earthenware, pottery, and stoneware that issued from the Zanesville area from the 1800s to the present is truly monumental.

One annual production report was recorded in 1868 by C.C. Russell in his booklet *Zanesville as a Place of Residence.* "There were six factories making stoneware and other pottery in Zanesville, exporting a total of 705,000 gallons of pottery ware yearly."

An 1873 book published by the Board of Trade states, "It is [pottery items] conveyed by the [rail] car load to distant states and by boats to 11 points on the Ohio and Mississippi rivers," with output estimates listed as a million and a half gallons.

According to the March 8, 1873, issue of the *Zanesville Daily Courier* which published the result of the recently completed ninth U.S. Census, Muskingum County contained 31 businesses involved in the clay industry, employing 97 people and with annual output worth of nearly $80,000. The decades of the 1880s and 90s would see even more potteries starting up, such as Weller and McCoy, to join Owens and Roseville in the Zanesville area.

By 1891 the Zanesville kilns were producing four million gallons for sale. The wares were shipped by steamboat down river to points as far south as New Orleans, and by rail from Michigan to Nebraska. Local and regional demand were also very high, and many flat bed barges fully loaded with potters' ware drifted down river to supply individual customers. The barges stopped at every town and settlement along the Muskingum and Ohio rivers, not returning until the entire stock of pots were sold.

The development of the American ceramic industry and its golden age are a result of dedicated men and women who worked the potteries, the early ceramists who experimented with clay bodies, glaze formulae, and kiln development. The romantic notion of epiphany in a production pottery is nonsense for the most part — the fact is that it was a dangerous, dirty, hot, unpleasant way to earn a living. In the nineteenth century, stoneware containers and utilitarian pottery items were a necessity, but very soon the potter's craft would develop into an art.

Although Rookwood Pottery was located in Cincinnati, its artistic influence was felt throughout Ohio and the rest of the country. The Arts and Crafts movement adopted pottery as one of its mediums of expression. Other Zanesville potters also began producing art ware lines alongside the previous utilitarian ware.

Zanesville, Ohio, was once the home of 31 potteries and tile factories. One of the country's oldest and the last surviving Zanesville pottery that dates from these times is the Zanesville Stoneware Company, in continuous operation at the same location for over 100 years until December 3, 1990, when it was totally destroyed by fire.

After the destruction of the factory the business moved to its present location at 1107 Muskingum Avenue and continues the modern production of Stoneware Planters and Clay Pots today. Many of the photos and catalogs used in this book survived the fire, housed in the company safe, others did not. In some cases the only copies of the destroyed articles remain in private hands. Care has been taken to find the best quality materials available for this project. The story begins in 1893 with the grandly conceived but ill-fated Ohio Encaustic Tile Company.

6

Ohio Encaustic Tile Company

Clay, the vast natural resource so abundant in the Ohio valley area, was the raw ingredient for the potter's craft. This high quality clay would be used to produce world class pottery. Located in east central Ohio, Zanesville was in the heart of this clay-producing region, and home to many local potters and small potteries producing stoneware.

Early uses of stoneware items were for everyday living, utilitarian items such as stoneware crocks, jugs, cuspidors, and other practical objects.

With the affluence of the Gilded Age came an interest in the finer things in life. In the 1850s American business concerns began importing European finery. Particularly English pottery and tile were of superior quality and thought to be unequaled by domestic companies.

The Victorian decorating ethic demanded embellishment, increasing the popularity and importation of English tile. Fireplace mantles were finished with inlaid tile not only because of their durable, fire-resistant qualities but also the esthetic handmade surface. Tile is rugged and was used for elegant flooring and wall paneling decorations highly appreciated by the Arts and Crafts movement.

This popularity attracted the attention of domestic entrepreneurs eager to end the monopoly that English firms held on the American market.

Established in 1874, American Encaustic Tiling Company of Zanesville, Ohio, was one of the early U.S. producers of tile, with a reputation for quality. A very profitable concern, the company caught the attention of one Zanesville merchant, Samuel Elbert.

Samuel Elbert specialized in toys and notions and sold these goods from his shop on North

Downtown Zanesville, circa 1880s. Main and Fifth Street area near Samuel Elbert's novelty shop.

Fifth Street in Zanesville. In March 1883, Elbert enlisted the help of F.J.L. Blandy, A.P. Clark, G.M. Jewett, and L.D. Sandel in a new venture. With no experience or expertise in tile manufacture, they formed the Ohio Encaustic Tile Company as a speculative business venture.

The new enterprise was incorporated on June 27, 1883, with $50,000 of listed capital stock. Officers of the corporation were George M. Jewett, president; C.C. Hildreth, vice president; F.J.L. Blandy, secretary; and Alvah P. Clark, treasurer and general manager.

In the summer of 1883, stock in the company was offered for sale to investors and plans for the pottery were finalized. A June 28, 1883 *Courier* article announced, "It is proposed that we send to England for such material as cannot be manufactured here, and workmen are to be brought from that country in the fall, to arrive in Zanesville in October. The establishment of another tile works will afford work to many

skilled and unskilled laborers."

An ideal location was found, and owner Samuel C. Haver was offered $1,600 for the former stone quarry lot. This must have been the total amount in the treasury, for the remainder of the $2,100 asking price was solicited by private subscription.

Located on the corner of Woodlawn and Coopermill Road and complete with rail connection to the Cincinnati & Muskingum Valley Railway Company, with the acquisition of this property the search for an ideal building site for the construction of their state-of-the-art pottery ended.

October 1883 saw the start of construction of a pottery complex on the site. Everything was planned except who would actually be in charge of the technical and production side of the operation. This lack of expertise among the principals would prove fatal. The person they were searching for would be required to oversee all areas of

Early factory photo.

Front of factory in early photo.

the new company. This demanded someone with a comprehensive background in the difficult craft of tile making.

Native English tilemaker Henry Bagley was chosen for this position. Bagley was hired in the fall of 1883 to set up and supervise tile production for the Ohio Encaustic Tile Company. He had arrived in the Zanesville area in about 1881 to work for the American Encaustic Tiling Company.

Elbert and Blandy would not live to see the results of their labors since both died in the harsh winter of 1883 – 1884.

Louis DeRoche Sandel, a printer by trade, assumed Blandy's former position of secretary. Despite setbacks and the untimely death of two of the original founders, by the following spring of 1884 four large brick buildings and two smaller wooden ones were completed. They housed two round periodic kilns for bisque firing and two rectangular kilns for glaze firing along with clay grinding mills, fire pump, and other tile making machinery. Located next to the C&MV

Railroad line, the company would have easy access to rail for shipping goods.

In May 1884 newspapers heralded the fact that the business would employ 50 people and operate on large scale as soon as all the equipment was installed. The first president of the tile works was George M. Jewett, but the management of the firm was the responsibility of Alvah P. Clark who held the positions of treasurer and general manager.

In 1885 E.G. Bowen replaced Jewett as president and Clark became secretary. Henry Bagley, master tilemaker, was not up to the task of overseeing the entire tile works, production had been inconsistent to say the least, and the company's financial position was not improving. Bagley was either discharged or quit the company and returned to England with his family in February of 1885, taking his expertise in tile making with him.

Bagley's departure was not good for the Ohio Encaustic Tile Company, and its decline contin-

Above and below: Examples of Ohio Encaustic Tile, showing factory marking.

ued through the next year.

An announcement in the *Zanesville Daily Courier* February 2, 1886, issue states C.C. Hildreth, A.W Train, A.P. Clark, G.M. Jewett, and L.D. Sandel had been elected to the board of directors of the Ohio Encaustic Tile Company.

A.P. Clark resumed his former occupation of drug store manager in early February 1886.

By June 1886 the tile factory was no longer in operation, and the site was abandoned.

The tile works lasted only a few years and examples of their tiles are difficult to find. Some of the titles were installed in the Zanesville City Jail and also one of the local hotels. Many of the tiles were dunted, or bowed, in the kilns, which attests to the difficulty of producing a flat, square perfect tile.

By the following December, legal problems beset the ill-fated tile plant. In a court judgment in favor of A.W. Train, executor of the F.J.L. Blandy estate, v. the Ohio Encaustic Tile Company, a $2,702.51 property lien was issued by M.M. Granger, attorney on behalf of A.W. Train. The property was ordered to be sold at auction to pay the encumbrance.

The sheriff of Muskingum County conducted that sale at 1:00 p.m. January 22, 1887, at the front door of the Zanesville courthouse. Attendance must have been good, and the *Zanesville Daily Courier* recorded the temperature as a balmy 56 degrees.

The property and equipment, including engine and boiler, six tile presses and dies, saggers, steam slip kiln, and glaze mills were purchased at Sheriff Bethel's sale for $6,005 by Edgar Bowen. Bowen was representing the interests of Wheeler Stevens, a successful wholesale grocer, who planned to set up a cigar factory and tobacco warehouses on the property.

Cigar manufacturing was big business in Zanesville, and Wheeler Stevens' idea of supply-

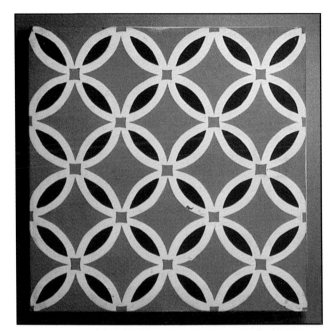 

These are some of the only known existing tiles, showing typical colors used.

ing his customers' tobacco needs from his own factory was a good one. But with all the mechanical necessities of a tile factory now at his disposal, stoneware manufacture would be a logical enterprise. Plans changed and the former tile works would not be converted into tobacco factory, but into a pottery producing a variety of stoneware articles.

E.G. Bowen and Company

The former Ohio Encaustic Tile Company property had been appraised at $8,500, due in part to the real estate boom the Zanesville area was enjoying, proximity of three railways passing the buildings, and the substantial brick buildings and equipment left on the property. The auction price of $6,005 must have seemed a bargain.

Wheeler Stevens' role other than financial seems shadowy in this firm. E.G. Bowen formed a partnership with Alvah P. Clark, former general manager of the Ohio Encaustic Tile Company enterprise.

The new firm of E.G. Bowen and Company took over the site and began producing a commercial stoneware line including jugs, chamber pots and cuspidors. Some insight into the operation is advanced in an August 24, 1887, *Courier* article, "Some months ago E.G. Bowen and A.P. Clark organized what is known in business circles as the Zanesville Stoneware Company. The operation has been in business for several weeks and yesterday first sales were made to dealers in this city. While the first burn is not as perfect as desired, the ware is pronounced by all who examined it as handsome as has been produced in this valley." By 1888 the operation employed 27 people.

Advertising cards, circa 1890.

The Zanesville Stoneware Company

History

In order to secure more capital for expansion, E.G. Bowen and Company would reorganize January 17, 1889, and incorporate January 19, 1889, as the Zanesville Stoneware Company. Shares of capital stock were offered for sale to the public from the office of John R. Stonesipher.

Bowen held 128 shares and Clark 10 shares. Purchasing further interest in the new firm was Wheeler Stevens, wealthy Zanesville businessman and president of Wheeler Stevens Wholesale Grocery Company. Stevens invested in 134 shares along with fellow grocers Dennis Hayes, vice president of Stevens Wholesale Grocery, and Milman Linn, secretary/treasurer of the grocery, both with three shares each. Milman Linn was the trusted younger cousin of Stevens. Other investors were F.H. Herdman and John C. Harris with one share each. The new company assumed the business of E.G. Bowen and Company from the first of that year.

Wheeler Stevens was looking for new ways to expand his wholesale grocery enterprise. With the placement of Linn to oversee this new financial investment, the stoneware business could generate a good business, insuring a steady supply of stoneware storage jars, crocks, preserving jars, chamber pots, and other essential stoneware goods sold from Stevens' Zanesville store front located at 169 Main St. in Zanesville.

The first line-up of officers of the Zanesville Stoneware Company was E.G. Bowen, president and treasurer; Milman Linn, vice president; and A.P. Clark, secretary. Twenty people were employed at the factory, and three muffle updraft kilns were used in production. Clays were acquired locally and transported to the pottery by horse-drawn wagon. The same clay deposits were used for a century, consistently firing to a yellow buff color.

1890s photograph of the Zanesville Literary Club. Members included J.B. Owens, A.P. Clark, and M.H. Linn, standing far right.

Office door, corner of Woodlawn and Pershing (Coopermill Road), circa 1930. From left: Francis Linn, Milman H. Linn Sr., Vincent B. Linn, Milman H. Linn Jr.

Milman Hart Linn Sr., circa 1930.

Milman H. Linn Sr.

At the 1889 annual board meeting, first-year sales were reported at only $17,549. Wheeler Stevens, disappointed with the annual earnings, decided to change the management and promoted Milman Linn to president of Zanesville Stoneware. Linn was working both at the pottery and Stevens' grocery as bookkeeper. With the urging of Stevens, Linn would devote all his time to the stoneware business. Determined to make more of a success of the new business, Stevens brought into the firm another one of his grocery employees, W.T. Beach, at the same time.

By 1891, the company occupied a prominent position in the pottery market. A local newspaper described their wares as a general line of stoneware of the highest quality, excellent in regards to shape, finish, and durability. Some of the early product line included milk pans, churns, Dutch pots, spittoons, and a unique stoneware water filter. These were available in both salt glaze and black Albany slip glaze.

The 1893 Zanesville City Directory lists the officers of the Zanesville Stoneware Company as M.H. Linn, president; F.H. Herdman, vice president; A.P. Clark, secretary.

In 1893 Professor Edward Orton Jr., a noted ceramics expert and developer of the pyrometric firing cone, wrote an article describing the Zanesville Stoneware complex as employing 25 people, with a production capacity of 900,000 gallons annually, and using three kilns. Orton reported the company was the first pottery in Ohio to use the newly developed muffle updraft kiln.

Early factory photo, circa 1895.

Early factory photo, circa 1895.

A muffle updraft kiln contains a refractory chamber inside the fuel burning kiln. This muffle chamber contains the pottery to be fired and is designed to protect the pottery from the open flame. A more controlled burn can take place, resulting in a superior finished product.

With increased business the company needed to expand, and ground was broken on a new, immense frame warehouse in September 1894.

Edward Orton Jr. established the Pyrometric Cone Company in 1896. Firing cones could determine the precise temperature inside the kiln, eliminating the guesswork of the previous methods in which Noble metal rods made of brass or bronze are inserted into the kiln and observed until they melted to determine the ceramic maturation temperature. Widespread use of the Orton Standard Pyrometric Cone advanced the entire ceramic industry. With firing cones, kilns could be monitored and maintained with consistent firing temperatures; higher quality wares were easier to produce, and production increased.

Spurred by the influence of the Arts and Crafts and Mission movements to meet the market demand for quality mass-produced pottery and new developments in ceramic technology, the 1890s saw an increase in the numbers of potteries starting up in Ohio, many in the "Clay City" area. The S.A. Weller pottery in 1893, Arc-en-Ciel and Peters and Reed in 1903 were among these.

In 1899, Alvah Clark sold his shares in the Zanesville Stoneware Company to W.B. Cosgrove. Clark then formed the Ohio Pottery Company in the J.B. Owens addition next to the Zanesville subdivision of Brighton.

Advertising card, circa 1890.

Imprint from company envelope.

Linn and Beach acquired the stock of the aging Wheeler Stevens. About 1910 Cosgrove sold his shares to Edward M. DeVol, plant superintendent. In a few years DeVol was company vice president.

The success of the local art potteries did not go unnoticed by Zanesville Stoneware. Limited art ware pieces were produced as early as 1889 at the company. Around 1910 they produced a full line of stoneware items and began manufacturing their first line of garden pottery, bird baths, vases, and jardinieres. A beautiful matte green glaze was developed for the art ware line by ceramists W.T. Beach and E.M. Devol. Matte green was one of two glazes offered in the #4 catalog from 1912, the other being a light cream color. Other matte colors listed in an early catalog include robin egg blue and stone gray.

Milman Linn loved to travel, not only throughout this country and adjacent countries, but also extensively in Europe, making the arduous crossing by sea on four occasions. Italy was his favorite destination, and he drew on this exposure to the classic Italian pottery forms for inspiration in his pottery lines. He occasionally brought back pottery purchased in Europe to be used as reference pieces. Designs based on Linn's ideas were prepared by his employees and the models, molds, and glazes were produced in-house.

The cast figural Rubble Ware line was inspired by Linn's trip to Rome. Watching the local peasants gather wood and water with the ancient backdrop of cobblestones and overgrown rubble prompted one of the more artistic designs the company produced.

Stoneware selection, circa 1889.

The antique Italian designs proved to be a favorite, and a press molded line of Italian flower pots were introduced, from 9 to 21 inches in size. Outside ornamentation was quite fashionable in this Arts and Crafts period, and most of the Zanesville area potteries produced inexpensive, sturdy lines of Garden Ware for outside use. The Zanesville Stoneware Company excelled in the manufacture of huge stoneware pots which were hand thrown in sizes from 20 inches to 26 inches and sold for $12 to $30 each.

In 1913 a devastating flood hit the Zanesville area. The rivers that were so vital in the development of Zanesville now threatened the town with complete destruction. Water surrounded homes in the old Putnam section of town. Eventually the whole area became flooded, forcing homeowners to evacuate to higher ground.

The Zanesville Stoneware Company buildings were situated above the flood waters and became homes as crowds of displaced people fleeing the disaster arrived. With the the rail lines at hand, food and needed supplies could be brought to the refugees. The Ohio National Guard was sent in and stationed at the plant during this ordeal. As supplies came in by train, they were distributed from the factory rail siding by the Ohio National Guard with the assistance of the company officers. To relax, off-duty guardsmen pressed kilns into service as a smoking parlor. The plant was closed for the following month as flood damage was cleared.

1913 flood aftermath.

18

1913 flood aftermath.

With the end of World War I, the company's glaze lines were expanded to include various colored gloss glazes and two-color "overflow" combinations. The 1920s issued in a new age with bolder color and intensity. Responding to this post war attitude, new multicolored glazes were used by the company. Tea pots, creamers, and covered bowls were added to the line of products as consumer demand increased after the war's end. The booming economy spurred sales not only in the United States but internationally. Zanesville Stoneware's sales extended to South America and Cuba. The company employed 100

men in pottery production. Items manufactured included stoneware filters, jardinieres, assorted flower pots, and even cuspidors.

The new glazes were developed and manufactured in-house by ceramist Edward M. DeVol throughout the 1920s. One of the first signature glazes Zanesville Stoneware developed was zasko, a light gray glaze with a dark blue runover. Some early examples of zasko are die-stamped with the word ZASKO in the bottom.

Most production pieces were stamped on the base with shape numbers.

Large hand turned pottery is what Zanesville

Lawrence F. Pickrull, master potter.

fashion called topping, throwing the top on one wheel and the base on another, then adding the top to the base to form large pots. He produced some of the company's largest pots, hand signing some of his favorites. Hank also had a stamp made of his last name and used it to mark pieces.

Hank was the last hand turner employed at the firm, retiring after years of turning in 1946. The largest hand thrown pot Pickrull made was 6 feet high. Five were created and two were used as part of a float representing the remaining area potteries: S.A. Weller, Burley Clay Products, Gonder Ceramic Arts, La Pere Pottery Company, Ohio Porcelain Company, Roseville Pottery, Shawnee Pottery, and Zanesville Stoneware Company. The float was created for the Zanesville sesquicentennial celebration on October 7, 1947. The two giant pots that were used for the float were sold after the parade for $50. The other three were destroyed, along with their molds, in the factory fires 40 years later.

In 1921 the company purchased a tract of land for future development near the fairgrounds, but it was never used as a factory site. Milman Linn 2nd, "Junior," returned from graduate school to join the firm in 1925. Arthur and Alfred DeVol, the sons of E.M. DeVol, joined the company in the 1930s as ceramic engineer and sales manager, respectively.

According to a 1930s advertisement in the *Crockery and Glass Journal*, five display rooms were located across the country. In New York, W.W. Jacobs, 25 Fifth Avenue; Chicago, J.B. Finn, 130 N. State Street; Seattle, Stearns & Hagen, 403 Holland Building; Boston, H.P. & H.F. Hunt and Company, 72 Summer St.; and the company showroom at the Zanesville factory complex.

In 1932 a new gas-fired Harrop tunnel kiln was built for the Zanesville Stoneware Company by the Cleveland engineering firm of Allied Engineering. The kiln was enlarged in 1952 to a capacity of 21 cars.

Stoneware is known for. These massive pots, once only used in the garden, proved popular inside too. Sand jars and oil jars were sold to theaters, offices, hotels, and show rooms for use in their lobbies. Some were used as planters, some for ash receptacles, and others as an artistic statement in their own right.

Hand turning a spinning 100-pound lump of clay calls for special craftsmen. The company employed many turners through out their history, but the man that made Zanesville Stoneware famous with his large clay creations was L.F. Pickrull.

"The star of the hand turners," is the response I received when I asked current company president Bud Linn about Lawrence F. "Hank" Pickrull. Pickrull worked as a big-ware hand turner in the 1920s.

He turned these huge pots in a two-piece

20

Milman H. Linn, guiding force behind the Zanesville Stoneware Company, passed away on August 11, 1940. In an article from *The American Ceramic Society*, September 15, 1943, recounting Linn's fifty years as a progressive potter, states, "Milman H. Linn was a progressive potter, one of the last of the 'old guard' of manufacturers who did so much to make Zanesville nationally famous as a pottery center. He kept his factory operations modern, investing in labor saving machines. As new technologies developed, they were incorporated into the process. He followed the transition from hand thrown stoneware crocks, jugs, jars, and churns for farm and town households to the cast and jiggered utility, cooking, and architectural stoneware of today, pio-

First-place float representing the eight remaining Zanesville potteries, featuring large pots made by Zanesville Stoneware, 1947.

neering in the transition from early salt and slip glaze to the opaque and colored Bristol glazes to the high-gloss lead-fritted glaze compounds."

Upon his death Milman Hart Linn bequeathed to his 40 employees of 10 years or more $100 each from his estate. The company stock was passed to his four children. His sons, Milman Linn Jr. became the company president; Vincent Linn, vice president; and Francis Linn, sales manager.

Third-generation seventeen-year-old Milman "Bud" Linn 3rd began working his way from the bottom up, starting his career in ceramics as a "dirt dog," cleaning the factory and doing other unpleasant tasks, but he was fascinated by the transforming processes taking place within the kilns and the anticipation of opening the kiln door and seeing the color that had appeared on the ware. By 1957 he was general manager and director of the company.

As World War II approached and submarine activity made sea travel dangerous, supplies and suppliers were unable to cross the Atlantic. Carbone Company of Boston asked the company to reproduce Country Fare, a flatware dish set, that had been previously produced for them by a Swedish company.

During World War II the company produced stoneware chemical developing tanks for the Eastman Kodak Company. Water filters were used for water purification in remote locations. These filters were exported to Africa, South America, Cuba, and the Caribbean Islands. Domestic consumer items were smaller Art Deco pieces and large heavy garden pots.

An article written by Norris Schneider for the *Times Signal* dated September 8, 1957 states, "The company now manufactures approximately 500 different pottery items. In addition to the popular Hostess line of dinnerware including 70 items, produced for the Carbone Company Inc. of Boston, Massachusetts," Schneider adds, "there are attractive articles of garden pottery, industrial stoneware of the finest quality, and pottery specialties of every kind. It is a tribute to the judgment and efficiency of the Z. S. C. executives that they have continued to operate and carry on the ceramic traditions of this city, long after the jolly wheels of older and larger potteries have stopped turning and the kilns have become cold." The officers are listed as Milman Linn, president; Alfred DeVol, vice president; Russell Harris, secretary; and Vincent Linn, treasurer.

50th anniversary company picnic, 1939.

22

In the 1960s Bud Linn began designing a popular line of stoneware planters and jardinieres with a jet age look; these he called "Stoneage Modern." His influences were California pottery and architectural pottery, a simple yet stylized futurist form. These opened up new markets for the business. By 1962 the Country Fare hostessware line included over 60 pieces from coffee pots, mugs, cruets, cups and saucers, to a full line of bakers' bowls and covered casserole sets. The hostessware was sold F.O.B. from the Zanesville Stoneware factory, as well as being distributed by Carbone Company Inc.

The century mark was reached in 1989 by Zanesville Stoneware Company. This was celebrated in The Times Recorder article dated January 22, 1989, "The Zanesville Stoneware Marks 100th Year." At that time Milman Linn Jr. was chairman of the board; his brother Vincent, vice president; son Milman Linn 3rd, president; and grandson Andrew Linn was sales manager and board member. The company, proud of its heritage and tradition, was producing larger stoneware items mainly for the lawn and garden trade, the average piece weighing 20 lbs. with a 12-inch diameter. Larger imported pottery often arrived broken. Zanesville Stoneware capitalized

on this and produced these large jardinieres domestically. Many Zanesville pots have appeared on Hollywood films as period set decorations. The company employed 13 at this time but were able to produce more goods due to greater productivity from the employees and a shuttle kiln that had been installed four years earlier. Milman H. Linn Jr., active in the community and a lifetime resident of Zanesville, died on November 21, 1990. His son Milman H. "Bud" Linn 3rd became chairman of the board and majority shareholder.

Only twelve days later, on December 3, 1990, at about 11 p.m., a door on the shuttle kiln opened prematurely as the temperature was at its maximum, over 2000 degrees. The following inferno engulfed the 100-year-old pottery. Local firefighters battled the blaze and had it contained by 3 a.m., but sadly it was too late. The fire had destroyed the entire pottery complex. Only the contents of the old company safe survived, a few photos, documents, and some of the early catalogs. A decision not to rebuild on the site was made due to lack of available land on the corner lot for any expansion.

The company is in existence today, despite the destruction of the factory. The business

1960s trade show featuring Stoneage Modern planters.

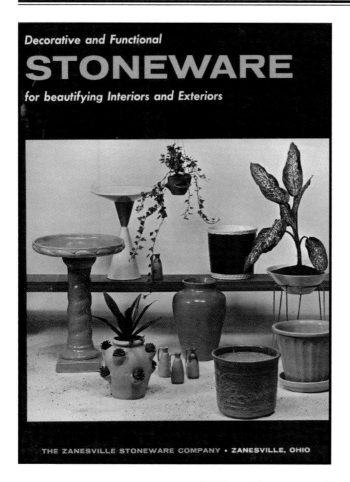

1960s catalog covers show Stoneage Modern look.

Andrew Linn, Bud Linn, and Milman Linn Jr. are shown at the 1989 Entrepreneur of the Year Awards.

moved to its present location on Muskingum Avenue and continues the modern production of ceramic planters and clay pots for the lawn and garden and interior plantscape industries, with Milman Linn 3rd as chairman of the board and president, and Andrew Linn, vice president and sales manager.

The Zanesville Stoneware Company is one of the oldest potteries in the country, and the last surviving pottery that dates from Zanesville's golden era of pottery production — "In continuous operation without a strike, or shutdown longer than necessitated by repairs or building additions," producing pottery at the same location for over 100 years until the fire.

24

Aftermath of the fire. (Photos taken December 5, 1990.)

Production

Stoneware is a single fire glazed pottery fired between 2150 and 2350 degrees Fahrenheit, a process which fuses the glazes and green clay body together into a vitreous state. From the beginning, Zanesville Stoneware used clays of local origin, a gray surface clay dug by hand from the Saltillo area of Perry County, Ohio, and transported to the pottery by horse-drawn wagon.

Zanesville used no additional clay aging process that many other potteries employed. The raw clay is first mixed with water in a plunger, producing a slurry. The slurry is filtered through a fine sieve and filter press to remove impurities. Next the excess water is drained off and the resulting mixture is placed into the pug mill, where the air is removed and the clay is mixed to the right consistency. The clay is then cut into properly sized pieces for hand turning or water is added for slip casting.

Photograph of factory employee, 1989.

Pottery production took place on the second floor where most large pieces were hand turned. Two other methods were also used. Pieces were formed with the use of jiggers or jollys where thicker consistency clay was formed by pressing into a rotating mold. Slip casting was used for the smaller items. Slip is a thinner mix of clay which is poured into plaster molds. The filled molds are allowed to set overnight during which the water is absorbed into the plaster. Next the greenware is taken out of the mold, dried to leather hard, and fetteled, which means cleaned of mold marks and imperfections, and placed on the drying racks.

The racks were suspended on ceiling-mounted tracks that are conveyed throughout the factory in a circular manner, slowly moving forward over a 24-hour period, allowing the waste heat from the first floor kilns to dry the pots in earnest and moving them back to where they started, dried to chalk hard. Next the pottery is glazed. Glazes were made in-house and applied by either spraying and dipping. In the early years the pots were hand dipped into the glaze solution; later the glaze was sprayed onto the piece. After additional air drying, the pottery was fired, maturing both the clay body and glaze at the same time.

If the greenware was not dry enough, the trapped moisture would boil in the kiln's heat and cause the piece to explode in the kiln with an incredible force, doing damage to other pieces and the kiln itself. With stoneware, any impurities in the clay, like coal, will push out of the clay during firing, resulting in blemishes and eruptions in the glaze finish.

Zanesville Stoneware used both a tunnel kiln and a shuttle kiln. In a shuttle kiln the shuttle car filled with glazed pottery is placed into the kiln, and the kiln is sealed. After firing the doors are opened and the shuttle car is backed out of the chamber. In a tunnel kiln shuttle cars pass through the chamber continuously and emerge as finished product at the opposite end. Stoneware using only one firing is less expensive to produce. Storage and shipping were located on the first floor along with kilns. In the early days, when a customer's order was finished, it was packed in straw and placed in wooden crates for rail shipment.

The same clay deposits were used by the

Photographs of factory employees, 1989.

Zanesville logo letterhead, 1922.

Zanesville pottery for a century, and pieces made from this clay were fired to semi-vitreous at 2000°F to a yellow buff color that aids in identifying Zanesville pieces. Some early pieces are not bottom glazed. Most slip cast pieces are bottom glazed and show stilt marks on the bottom of the pot.

Hundreds of designs were produced through the years, from florists vases to a full garden line. Lamp bases to accommodate either oil and electricity were made, but lamps were not assembled at the factory. Being a wholesale pottery, Zanesville Stoneware sold to many companies,

and contract production is responsible for many specific items such as lamps, dinnerware, humidifiers, and vases for chain florist shops.

Glaze development continued through the years as varieties of gloss and matte color were added to their production line. In the early years the color palette was limited to the traditional Albany slip and salt type glazes.

Around 1910 the Zanesville Stoneware company started manufacturing their first line of garden pottery. A beautiful matte green glaze was developed for this line by W.T. Beach and E.M. DeVol.

With their entry into the floral and decorative markets around 1912, matte green, light cream and mahogany glazes were offered. Catalog #5 shows robin egg blue, stone gray, rough stone, and cement finishes.

Zasko Ware with a unique blue over gray drip glaze appears in Catalog #7. Catalog #8 shows an increase in experimentation with Bristol white and the announcement of assorted glazes. A variety of matte colors, rose, lavender, dark blue, and light blue, were listed in Catalog #9 along with new gloss colors, green, rose, lavender, black.

The supplement to Catalog #9 includes mottled buff and mottled rose. In Catalog #10,

Early photograph of Zanesville Stoneware potters.

dark blue over gray and royal blue are added.

The supplement to #10 lists new lighter shades of blue, green, yellow, pink, green over gray, black over green, and black over matte green. Omar Ware is listed as buff with color splashes. Also introduced were Vulcan and Neptune, both two-tone glazes. Vulcan had a buff with orange tint, and Neptune had a dark green and copper look.

The names of the glazes got more imaginative through Catalog #11 as the selection included overflow and blended glazes; Montrose with rose mottling on an ivory background; azure, a light blue with a cloudy effect; Brunell, a brown with lighter shading and splashes; matte russet; matte royal blue; royal gloss blue; forest green overflow; green over russet; and dark blue over light blue. Additional gloss glazes were seacrest green and stardew blue.

Catalog #12 lists Bacorcy, a black flow over green; Vorosa, rose over ivory; Blumoro, a Moorish blue; Ruddiglow, red tone with lighter shading; Verdantone, green flow over gray base; Ebonello, yellow flow over black; and Ebonivor, a black flow over white.

By 1951 and Catalog #14-R, basic assorted colors were listed with white and overflows available at a 10 percent extra charge.

At first glance the strong qualities of Zanesville Stoneware pottery are often overlooked. It was not meant to make a statement to be shouted across a room; instead these simple forms and harmonious glazes are for a more personal inspection. They possess depth and subtlety for the eye and accompanying texture for the touch that is seldom seen in other items produced by similar production potteries of the time.

Variations of their glazes are numerous, as shades varied from batch to batch, but it must be said that new glazes were introduced on a regular basis with a degree of artistic spontaneity, with feeling for the changing taste of the consumer.

A select clientele spurred the demand for outdoor pottery. To be used in a garden setting the pieces must be of a scale that is in harmony with the surroundings. Craftsmanship, beauty, and a certain indestructibility are major considerations when pottery is exposed to the elements. Stoneware is ideally suited for this type of rugged use.

The influence of Linn's favorite country,

Italy, proved equally as attractive to customers, and a press-molded line of Italian flower pots and villa pots were introduced, ranging from 9 to 21 inches in size. This line was manufactured for nearly 100 years.

Outside ornamentation was quite fashionable in the Arts and Crafts period, and most of the Zanesville area potteries produced sturdy lines of garden ware for outside use. The Zanesville Stoneware Company excelled in producing huge stoneware pots, hand thrown in sizes from 20 to 28 inches and sold for $30 per dozen.

Large hand-turned pieces proved popular for interior use also. Sand jars and oil jars were sold to theaters, hotels, and other businesses for use in their lobbies. Some were used for plantings, some for ash receptacles, and others for artistic statements in their own right. Jardinieres and pedestal sets adorned many households, along with vases for cut flowers on the mantles.

Garden Ware

The building boom and prosperity of the 1920s, and the popularity of the Arts & Crafts, Bungalow, and Art Deco styles were the driving factors in the market for garden pottery. Garden pottery was large scale vases, urns, jars, and stands made to weather both indoor and outdoor use. I would place the beginning of this type of production in the early '20s, the high point and beginning of the end being around 1930. It seems Zanesville Stoneware's early garden pottery started out much like other companies of the area like Robinson Ransbottom, J.W. McCoy, Brush, Nelson McCoy, Burley & Winter, Roseville, and Weller and Owens.

A dark matte green glaze was in vogue and the shapes were Nouveau blended into Arts & Crafts. Forms included jar and pedestals, bowls, simple spill vases in many sizes, and a half-dozen or so large hand-turned oil jars. Stylistically, there is not much from this early period that breaks any new ground. Shapes tended to be classic and straightforward. Glazes tended to be single color matte and gloss in a limited range, a conservative but wise approach for a company which primarily had been producing utilitarian stoneware.

Zanesville Stoneware was one of five mid-line stoneware giants in the area; the others were

An exhibit by the Zanesville Stoneware Co. at the National Flower Show. Buffalo. N. Y.

An exhibit of Zanesville Stoneware at the National Flower Show in Buffalo N.Y., circa 1930.

Robinson Ransbottom, Brush, Nelson McCoy, and Burley & Winter. Interestingly, each company seemed to evolve their own individual specialties and strengths and become very successful in close proximity to one another. Robinson Ransbottom made its mark with a value oriented line of workhorse shapes and in fact, made well-designed, good quality early art ware. Primarily their shapes were slip cast and mass produced, however it should be noted that for a brief period in the early '30s, they experienced a renaissance of sorts and produced some very high quality hand-thrown, hand-decorated garden ware lines.

Brush had Al Cusic to design classic shapes, and early Brush glazes were better than average. Also in the early '30s, Brush did a special line of large garden pots with overdrip glazes or squeeze bag decoration. These were all cast or jiggered items. By the mid to late '30s, most of the large

pieces were discontinued from the line.

Nelson McCoy was a powerhouse art ware company, having a full-time design staff with talented designers such as Sidney and Leslie Cope and Walter Bauer. Nelson McCoy undoubtedly produced the widest variety of ware of any of the manufacturers in the area. A company strong point was large scale garden ware with many jardiniere and pedestal combinations, sand jars, oil jars, and planters. They made some hand-turned oil jars, but most were jiggered, with handles applied to the pot while in a green state. These large pieces were produced into the 1950s.

Burley & Winter, another major producer of utility stoneware, flirted with the art ware idea for a 10 – 15 year stretch. Their forms and glazes are the most unusual of the group. Their early forms show an originality and confident flair that you would not associate with a mid-line company. Their mottled glazes run the gamut from

30

flamboyant to sublime. Of particular note are their letter series large scale garden pots. Approximately a dozen shapes were manufactured — well-formed, hand-thrown, thick-walled pieces with much better than average mottled matte glazes, many of which had handles.

Of note also are the large scale pieces by Weller. Decidedly more high-end, Weller made exceptional hand-decorated garden pottery, tile, fountains, and animals, as well as medium-priced lines such as Graystone. Large hand-thrown pieces tended to be special order, high grade items, limited in production.

Zanesville Stoneware's contribution to this area is in its extensive hand-thrown line. In the early 1920s they must have experienced genuine success with their earlier attempts, for the number of large shapes seems to increase significantly. The man behind these pots was Lawrence F. "Hank" Pickrull, a talented and proficient technician. The sheer numbers of the styles and range of sizes produced suggest that Zanesville Stoneware had a significant piece of the burgeoning market. The quality of these pieces is excellent, the best value for dollar, which allowed Zanesville Stoneware to compete successfully for national business.

During the 1940s and 1950s, Country Fare hostess ware was produced by the pottery for Carbone Inc. of Boston, Massachusetts. By 1957 the company manufactured approximately 500 different pottery items, with many popular designs in continuous production throughout its history.

In the 1960s Bud Linn began designing a popular line of stoneware planters and jardinieres with a modern architectural style. With a "jet age" look, he called this line Stoneage Modern. His influences were California pottery and Architectural pottery, a simple yet stylized futurist form. By 1962 the Country Fare hostess

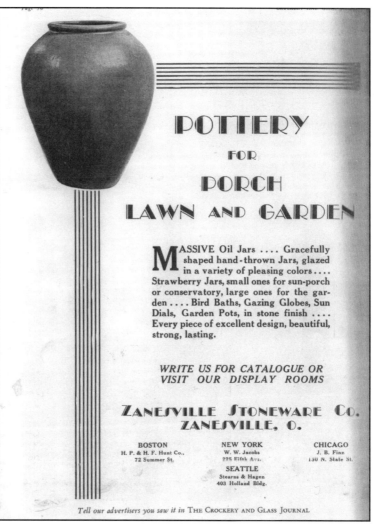

1930 advertisement in the *Crockery and Glass Journal*.

ware line included over 60 pieces from coffee pots, mugs, cruets, cups and saucer, a full line of bakers bowls, and covered casserole sets, sold F.O.B. from the Zanesville Stoneware plant.

After the fire and the company's relocation, production methods were changed to a state-of-the-art extrusion process. Now using a refined clay mix, simpler forms, and more mechanization that requires fewer personnel, Zanesville Stoneware is still a leading supplier of quality high-fired pottery planters.

1930 advertisements in the *Crockery and Glass Journal.*

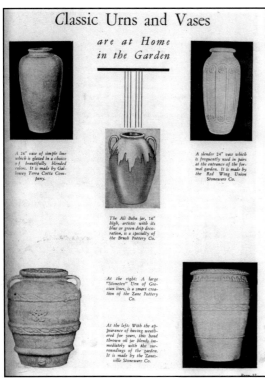

The Taller Members *of the* Garden Ware Family

ATTRATIVE GAZING GLOBE and Pedestal manufactured by the Zanesville Stoneware Co., Zanesville, O. This piece placed advantageously in your garden holds a fascination for all.

THE JAR AND PEDESTAL, above, is made in 8, 10 and 12 inch sizes by the Robinson Clay Product Co., 174 Fifth Ave., New York. They are also responsible for the new bird bath, shown below, which comes in gray stone finish only and is 23½ inches high—the bowl is 20 inches in diameter.

ARTCRETE PRODUCTS CO., Upper Darby P. O., Pa., are justly proud of their new gazing globe and pedestal, above, and their bird bath with detachable figure at the right. The gazing globe is 16 inches; the pedestal is 38 inches high; the bird bath is 38 inches high and 28 inches wide; the figure is 18 inches high.

Page 58

Flower Pots That Become a *Permanent Part* of the Garden

Here is a well designed garden pot from the Zane Pottery Co. It is their No. 40.

Large hand thrown oil jar, made in 10" and 24" sizes by the Zanesville Stoneware Co.

One of the popular Red Wing Union Stoneware Co.'s garden flower pots which is 10½" high and 17" in diameter.

A Villa Pot, 16" or 22" sizes, stone finish with a touch of green for decoration is an interesting number from the Zanesville Stoneware Co.

A classic design of simplicity and beauty makes these distinguished pieces, illustrated on either side, two of a large selection of such items made by the Galloway Terra Cotta Co.

1931 advertisements in the *Crockery and Glass Journal*.

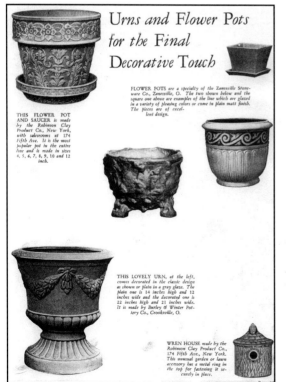

Urns *and* Flower Pots *for the* Final Decorative Touch

FLOWER POTS are a specialty of the Zanesville Stoneware Co., Zanesville, O. The two shown below and the square one above are examples of the line which are glazed in a variety of pleasing colors or come in plain matt finish. The pieces are of excellent design.

THIS FLOWER POT AND SAUCER is made by the Robinson Clay Product Co., New York, with salesrooms at 174 Fifth Ave. It is the most popular pot in the entire line and is made in sizes 4, 5, 6, 7, 8, 9, 10 and 12 inch.

THIS LOVELY URN, at the left, comes decorated in the classic design as shown or plain in a gray glaze. The plain one is 14 inches high and 12 inches wide and the decorated one is 22 inches high and 21 inches wide. It is made by Burley & Winter Pottery Co., Crooksville, O.

WREN HOUSE made by the Robinson Clay Product Co., 174 Fifth Ave., New York. This unusual garden or lawn accessory has a metal ring in the top for fastening it securely in place.

1931 advertisement in the *Crockery and Glass Journal*. The caption reads as follows:

Now that things are being done on a bigger scale, the Zanesville Stoneware Company has produced this enormous garden vase of high fired pottery ... it is mottled in effect. Don't you think this number is rather tempting? The pretty girls, who found no difficulty in squeezing into the large vase, will show you this and other Zanesville numbers, when you visit the display of W. W. Jacobs, 225 Fifth Ave., New York.

Zanesville Ware

Meeting the demand for pottery for porch, lawn and garden, the Zanesville Stoneware Co., Zanesville, O., have assembled a striking line of oil jars, of the hand-thrown variety in artistic colors, strawberry jars, bird baths, gazing globes, sun dials, flower pots and all the other items which go to make the garden, lawn and porch more inviting. The Zanesville line is shown in New York, Boston, Chicago, and Seattle.

1931 advertisement in the *Crockery and Glass Journal*.

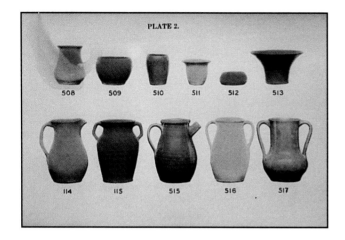

Three hand-tinted catalog pages, circa 1920.

25-year employee pin.

Aerial photo of the Zanesville Stoneware Company.

Marks and Identification

Zanesville Stoneware used a gray surface clay dug by hand from Perry County, Ohio. The same clay deposits were used for a century. This clay becomes semi-vitreous when fired at 2000°F, producing a yellow buff color that aids in identifying pieces. Some early pieces are not bottom glazed. Most slip cast pieces are bottom glazed with either a clear glaze or a primary glaze color and show stilt marks on the bottom of the pot.

Glazes were made in-house and applied by both spraying and dipping. In the early years the pots were hand dipped into the glaze solution, and later the glaze was sprayed onto the piece. Typical glaze imperfections are common with these stoneware pieces, created as a less expensive alternate to Rookwood, Roseville, and Weller products.

Around 1910 the company started manufacturing their first line of garden pottery and art ware in a beautiful matte green glaze. Other matte colors listed in an early catalog include robin egg blue and stone gray.

Production was a driving force and commercial customers who had items they wanted reproduced would have them copied and manufactured by Zanesville Stoneware and marked with the customer's name. This marking is stamped in the base in an oval pattern in italic letters. Many varieties of this mark have been found and are shown on the following four pages. Markings of regional florists can be found in different parts of the country, bearing this same type of lettering. Bisque pottery blanks were sold to Clewell Pottery in the 1920s and many appear with Clewell's Shrouded Bronze glaze.

Zanesville chose not to mark their products with any identification other than shape markings, a series of numbers and letter marks stamped into the bottom of the pot. Federal law required that imported pottery be marked, so to avoid being mistaken for inferior foreign goods, Zanesville used no maker mark for themselves for many years.

Mistaken identity has been the curse for collectors of this pottery due to these markings or the lack of them.

Stamped markings that have been uncovered include 1926 Philadelphia, Pa. Sesqui-centnl (sic); Country Fare Hostess ware line made for Carbone Co. Inc., Boston, Mass., also sold wholesale from Zanesville Stoneware factory in early 1960s; F.R. Depetris Better Flowers, a florist shop located in Newark, Ohio; Dutchess Cheese, New York; Henry Foster Finer Flowers, Fisher Bldg.

Made for Charles Mayer & Company, Indianapolis, a large Indiana retailer that offered a variety of goods to the public under their own label, a clue that a common link connected these similar appearing products, a single producer that acted as a jobber producing the wares that were being sold under company names other than their own; Marco Pottery Hand Made, small pottery located in Zanesville, Ohio, during the 1940s and 1950s.

The Old Pot Shop, Norwalk, Ct., known for its wonderful pottery items and sales to the multitudes of tourists that passed by Frank J. Duggan's shop on Westport Avenue insured the pottery spread to all parts of the country, only adding to the mystery of the true maker. (Zanesville pieces are sometimes called Norwalk Pottery and Duggan Pottery.) The fact was that Duggan, a colorful and talented potter and entertaining salesman, could sell more pottery than he could produce, and the bulk of his attributed pieces were purchased from the Zanesville Stoneware commercial line, stamped with the Old Pot Shop trade name, and sold to tourists along the Boston-Post Road.

Pickrull, Lawrence F. Pickrull in the 1920s worked as a large ware hand turner and produced some of the company's largest wares. Hand signing some of his favorites, he also had a stamp which he used until his retirement in 1946; USA, found on export pieces to Canada; Wally Frank, English firm specializing in tobacco products; ZASKO, some early examples of line are die stamped with the word ZASKO in the bottom an abbreviation of Zanesville Stoneware Co.; ZSC, in block letters, pottery began using this mark in the 1960s; circular Zanesville Stoneware, impressed mark used after the fire in 1990, still currently in use.

36

Country Fare.

F.R. Depetris Better Flowers.

Dutchess Cheese, New York.

Henry Foster Finer Flowers.

(Left) Made for Charles Mayer & Company, Indianapolis.

(Right) Wally Frank Ltd.

Marco Pottery Hand Made.

1926 Philadelphia, Pa., sesqui-centnl (sic).

Old Pot Shop, Norwalk, Ct.

In the 1920s, Lawrence F. Pickrull worked as a large ware hand turner and produced some of the company's largest wares. Hand signing some of his favorites, he also had a stamp made and used it to mark pieces until his retirement in 1946.

Raised marks, ⅝".

ZSC, in block letters.

Small number stamp, ¼".

Zasko.

Circular Zanesville Stoneware, impressed mark used from 1990 and still currently in use.

Large number stamp, ½".

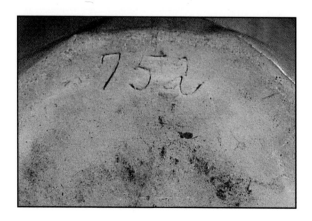

Hand incised mark.

(Left and above) Omar Ware paper label.

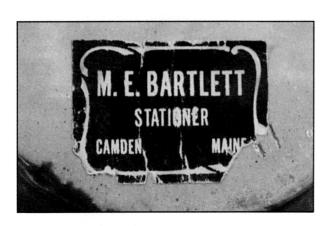

M.E. Bartlett applied paper label.

Speedway Pottery paper label, Tyrone, Pennsylvania.

Epi-curio ink stamp.

Malcolm's House and Garden Store, Baltimore, Md., Frederick, Md.

Glaze and Shape Identification

Shape #601, 5½", $75.00 – 95.00.

Shape #200, 9", $125.00 – 175.00.

Shape #309, 7½", $75.00 – 95.00

Shape #25, 9", $125.00 – 175.00.

(Top left) Shape #600, 12", $200.00 – 300.00;
(Top right) Shape #21, 10", $150.00 – 175.00;
(Bottom) Shape #1, 9", $75.00 – 100.00.

Detail of frieze, Jardiniere #600.

Top row, from left: Shape #22, 7", $100.00 – 125.00;
Shape #22, 7", $100.00 – 125.00;
Bottom row: Shape #22, 10", $125.00 – 175.00.

Shape #22, 7" with 16" pedestal, $300.00 – 350.00.

Jardiniere #0, 6", $75.00 – 100.00.

Jardiniere #103, 4½", $50.00 – 75.00.

(Left) Jardiniere #21, 10", $150.00 – 175.00; (right) jardiniere #21, 7", $100.00 – $125.00.

Shape #516, 9", $115.00 – 145.00.

**Shape #209, 3½",
$50.00 – 75.00.**

Top row, from left: Shape #830, 9", $100.00 – 150.00; Shape #21, 7", $100.00 – 125.00; Shape #322, 9", $100.00 – 125.00. Bottom row, from left: Shape #202, 6", $65.00 – 95.00; Shape #4, 8", $65.00 – 95.00; Shape #844, 9", $100.00 – 150.00; Shape #781, 8", $100.00 – 150.00.

Shape #49, 8½", $100.00 – 135.00;
Shape #C, 3½", $25.00 – 45.00.

From left:
Shape not marked,
Made for Charles
Mayer & Co.,
Indianapolis, 7",
$200.00 – 250.00;
Shape #D-18, 2¾"
dia., $10.00 – 25.00;
Shape #102, 8",
$100.00 – 125.00.

Shape #500, 7" dia., $125.00 – 175.00.

Shape #54, 6" x 7" dia., $50.00 – 75.00.

From left:
Shape #4, 8",
$65.00 – 95.00;
Shape #11, 7¼",
$150.00 – 175.00;
Shape #85, 7¼",
$65.00 – 95.00.

Top row, from left:
Shape #0, 6½", $75.00 – 100.00;
Shape #36, 11", $125.00 – 175.00;
Shape #791, 7", $65.00 – 95.00.

Bottom row, from left:
Shape #4, 8", $65.00 – 95.00;
Shape #756, 8", $75.00 – 100.00;
Shape #752, 7", $75.00 – 95.00.

Shape #729, 6", $50.00 – 75.00.

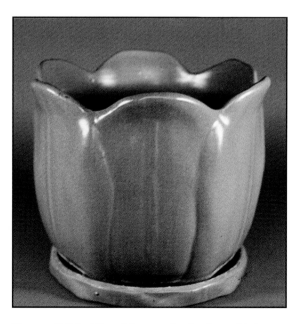

Shape #752, 7", with attached plate, $95.00 – 125.00.

Shape #720, 9", $125.00 – 175.00.

Shape #3V, 12", $125.00 – 175.00.

MATTE GREEN

Shape #108 WH, 15", $300.00 – 500.00.

Top row, from left: Shape #D-3, 3½", $15.00 – 20.00; Shape #734, 6", $65.00 – 95.00; Shape #D-14, 3½", $15.00 – 20.00. Bottom row, from left: Shape not marked, 4" x 6" dia., $35.00 – 55.00; Shape #26, 6", $35.00 – 55.00; Shape #60, 6", $65.00 – 95.00; Shape #510, 4½", $25.00 – 45.00.

Shape #F6, 4", $35.00 – 55.00.

Back row, from left: Shape #791,7", $125.00 – 145.00; Shape #203.9", $125.00 – 175.00; Shape #202, 12", $125.00 – 150.00; Shape #101, 8½", $125.00 – 165.00; Shape #202, 4½", $45.00 – 65.00. Front row, from left: Shape #104, 5", $95.00 – 125.00; Shape #105, 7", $100.00 – 135.00; Shape #0, 6", $75.00 – 100.00; Shape #0, 4", $65.00 – 95.00; Shape #0, 5", $70.00 – 90.00.

From left:
Shape #D1, 3½", $25.00 – 35.00;
Shape #D13, 5", $65.00 – 100.00;
Shape #D25, 2½", $20.00 – 30.00.

From left:
Shape #J, 12", $125.00 –
175.00; Shape #333, 6",
$35.00 – 45.00; Shape #795,
8½", $125.00 – 175.00.

From left:
Shape #509, 4", $45.00 – 55.00;
Shape not marked, 8½", $150.00 – 225.00;
Shape #508, 6", $75.00 – 95.00.

Shape #108, 18", $400.00 – 600.00.

Back row, from left: Shape #F1, 2½", $35.00 – 45.00; Shape #93, 6" dia., $45.00 – 55.00; Shape #523, Old Pot Shop, 9", $125.00 – 175.00; Shape #115, 9", $125.00 – 175.00; Shape #92, 5" dia., $45.00 – 55.00; Shape #511, 3½", $45.00 – 55.00. Front row, from left: Shape #8, 9" dia., $65.00 – $85.00; Shape #C, 5" dia., $30.00 – 40.00; Shape #207, 9½" dia., $75.00 – 95.00; Shape #E1, 5" dia., $30.00 – 40.00; Shape #509, 4", $45.00 – 55.00; Shape #510, 4½", $45.00 – 55.00.

Shape #799, 7", $145.00 – 195.00.

Shape #569, 11", $175.00 – 225.00.

Shape #720, lamp base, 9", $175.00 – 225.00.

Shape #J, lamp base, 12", $150.00 – 200.00.

Shape #1, 21" x 10" dia., $400.00 – 600.00.

Shape #2, 21" x 10" dia., $450.00 – 650.00.

Shape #102, 7", dark matte green, $125.00 – 150.00.

Top row, from left:
Shape #5, 8", $75.00 – 100.00;
Shape #11 ,7", $125.00 – 150.00;
Shape #102, 8", $135.00 – 165.00.

Bottom row, from left:
Shape #105, 7", $95.00 – 125.00;
Shape #101, 8½", $100.00 – 125.00;
Shape #513, 5", $65.00 – 85.00.

Top row, from left:
Shape #104, 5", $95.00 – 125.00;
Shape #4, 8", $95.00 – 125.00;
Shape #87, 8", $75.00 – 100.00;
Shape #510, 4¼", $45.00 – 55.00;
Shape #578, 2½", $15.00 – 25.00.

Bottom row, from left:
Shape #D-15, 2", $65.00 – 95.00;
Shape #D-14, 4¼", $45.00 – 55.00;
Shape #D-18, 1½", $15.00 – $20.00;
Shape #D-3, 4¼", $45.00 – 55.00;
Shape #D-15, 2", $65.00 – 95.00.

Shape #93, 6" dia., $45.00 – 55.00.

Top row, from left:
Shape #B-6, 11", $75.00 – 100.00;
Shape #851, 8", $45.00 – 55.00;
Shape #37, 12", $125.00 – 125.00.

Bottom row, from left:
Shape #762, 9", $150.00 – 200.00;
Shape #579, 9", $125.00 – 175.00;
Shape #B-5, 9½", $125.00 – 175.00.

Back row, from left: Shape #D12, 6½", Old Pot Shop, $55.00 –
75.00; Shape #517, 9", $150.00 – 200.00; Shape #509, 4", $50.00
– 60.00. Front row, from left: Shape #511, 3½", $50.00 – 60.00;
Shape #101, 8½", $125.00 – 150.00.

Shape #B3, 9", $125.00 – 175.00.

Pickrull hand-thrown shape #109, 21", $600.00 – 800.00.

Top row, from left: Shape #D-6, 5", $35.00 – 45.00; Shape #D-7, 4", $20.00 – 40.00; Shape not marked, 4", $45.00 – 55.00; Shape #F-1, 4", $25.00 – 35.00. Bottom row, from left: Shape #D-19, 9", $75.00 – 95.00; Shape #17, 6", $50.00 – 75.00; Shape #101, 8½", $125.00 – 150.00; Shape #D-4, 5½", $40.00 – 50.00; Shape #D-19, 9", $75.00 – 95.00.

Top row, from left:
Shape #579, 9", $125.00 – 175.00;
Shape #B-11, 11½", $125.00 – 150.00;
Shape #518, 9", $175.00 – 250.00.

Bottom row, from left:
Shape #103, 4½", $50.00 – 60.00;
Shape #795, 8½", $125.00 – 150.00;
Shape #827, 6", $75.00 – 100.00.

Shape not marked, Old Pot Shop, 12½", $350.00 – 500.00.

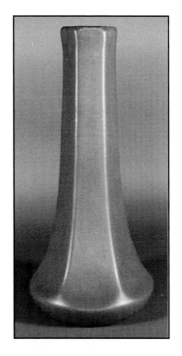

Shape #36, 12", $125.00 – 175.00.

Shape #B4, 11", $125.00 – 175.00.

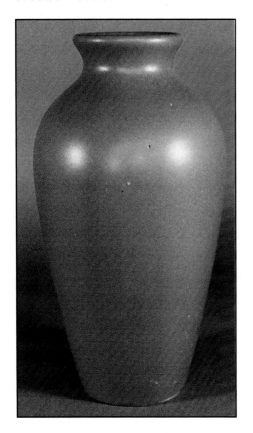

Shape #D23, 8", $100.00 – 125.00.

Shape #112, 21", $750.00 – 1,000.00.

Top row, from left:
Shape not marked, 8½",
$100.00 – 125.00;
Shape #17, 6", $40.00 – 75.00;
Shape #847, 17", 3 handles,
$250.00 – 400.00;
Shape #508, 6", $50.00 – 75.00;
Shape #D-18, 4½" dia.,
$20.00 – 35.00.

Bottom row, from left:
Shape #D26, 5", $35.00 – 45.00;
Shape #F1, 4", $35.00 – 45.00;
Shape #341, 4¼", $35.00 – 45.00;
Shape #509, 4½", $30.00 – 40.00;
Shape #D18, 5½" dia.,
$25.00 – 40.00.

Top row, from left: Shape #575, 3½" dia., $20.00 – 30.00, saucer #575, 5¾" dia., $10.00 – 20.00; Shape #D13, 5", $75.00 – 100.00; Shape #575, 3½", dia., $20.00 – 30.00, saucer #575, 5¾" dia., $10.00 – 20.00. Bottom row, from left: Shape #D14, 4¼", $20.00 – 30.00; Shape #D3, 3½", $20.00 – 30.00.

Shape #521, 12", fitted with lamp insert, $175.00 – 225.00.

Shape #513, 7¾" dia., $50.00 – 60.00.

Shape #785, lamp base, 8½",
$150.00 – 200.00.

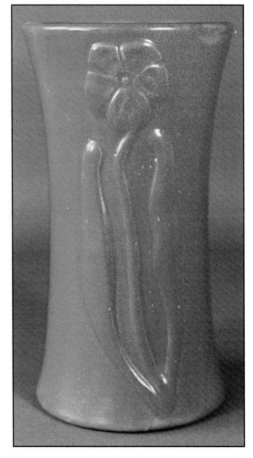

Shape #H7, 7" dia., $75.00 – 100.00.

Shape #576, 8½", $65.00 – 95.00.

From left:
Shape #B-7, 11", $125.00 – 175.00;
Shape #B-17, 7", $75.00 – 100.00;
Shape #795, 8½", $125.00 – 175.00.

From left:
Shape #BA-21, 3", $30.00 – 40.00;
Shape #332, 5", $45.00 – 55.00;
Shape #795, 8½", $125.00 – 175.00.

Shape #720, 12", $200.00 – 300.00.

Shape #J, 12", $200.00 – 300.00.

Clockwise from top left:
Shape #795, 8½",
$125.00 – 175.00;
Shape #795, 8½",
$125.00 – 175.00;
Shape #F1, 4", $30.00 – 40.00;
Shape #B17, 7",
$75.00 – 100.00.
Center: Shape #D26, 5",
$45.00 – 55.00.

Shape #510, 4½", $30.00 – 45.00.

Shape #558, 15", $450.00 – 650.00.

Shape #719, 27", $750.00 – 1,000.00.

Shape #108, 21", $300.00 – 400.00.

Shape #B11, 12½", $150.00 – 200.00.

From left:
Shape #576, 8½",
$65.00 – 95.00;
Shape #B-17, 7",
$75.00 – 100.00;
Shape #B-18, 10½",
$125.00 – 150.00.

Shape #523, 9", $125.00 – 150.00.

Gloss White

From left: Shape #333, 6", $45.00 – 55.00; Shape #845, 7½", $75.00 – 100.00; Shape #795, 9", $85.00 – 120.00.

Shape #BA10, 6" x 6" dia., $75.00 – 100.00.

Shape #230, 12", $75.00 – 120.00.

From left: Shape #576, 8½", $65.00 – 95.00; Shape #101, 8½", $75.00 – 100.00.

73

Shape #500, 7", $150.00 – 175.00.

Shape #J, 12", $150.00 – 175.00.

From left:
Shape #B-17, 7", $75.00 – 95.00;
Shape #4-VH, 12", $125.00 – 150.00;
Shape #576, 8½", $75.00 – 95.00.

From left:
Shape #F5, 4",
$30.00 – 45.00;
Shape #B13, 9",
$125.00 – 150.00.

Seacrest Green

Top row, from left: Shape #851, 8", $50.00 – 60.00; Shape #BA3, 6" dia., $50.00 – 60.00; Shape not marked, 4" x 6" dia., $40.00 – 50.00; Shape #336, 7½" x 9½", $50.00 – 60.00; Shape #869, 5¼", $45.00 – 55.00. Bottom row, from left: Shape #328, 6", $75.00 – 100.00; Shape #82, 6" dia., $50.00 – 75.00; Shape #865, 3", $35.00 – 45.00; Shape #95, 6" dia., $25.00 – 40.00; Shape #BA1, 8" dia., $30.00 – 40.00; Shape #868, 8½" x 11", $75.00 – 100.00.

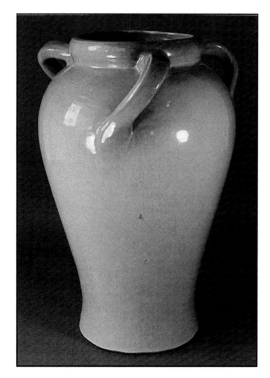

Shape #847, 16½", $250.00 – 350.00.

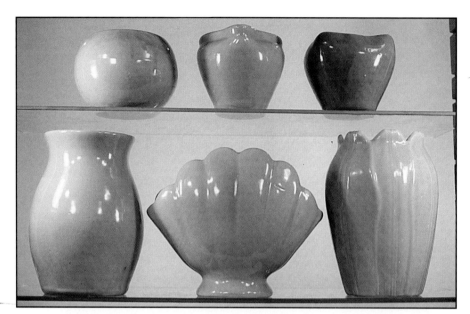

Top row, from left:
Shape not marked, 4",
$30.00 – 40.00;
Shape #F-4, 4", $30.00 – 40.00;
Shape #F-3, 4", $30.00 – 40.00.

Bottom row, from left:
Shape #829, 8½",
$85.00 – 100.00;
Shape #336, 8", $45.00 – 75.00;
Shape #307, 8½",
$100.00 – 125.00.

Detail of top #F-4.

From left:
Shape #330, 10", $75.00 – 90.00;
Shape #330, 8", $45.00 – 70.00.

From left:
Shape #B-9, 10",
$150.00 – 175.00;
Shape #2VH, 12",
$125.00 – 175.00;
Shape #B-7, 11",
$100.00 – 125.00.

Shape #B21, 18", $350.00 – 500.00.

Top row, from left:
Shape #4VH, 12", $125.00 – 175.00;
Shape #4VH, Old Pot Shop, 12",
$125.00 – $175.00.

Center row, from left:
Shape #829, 9", $100.00 – $125.00;
Shape #2VH, 12", $125.00 – 175.00;
Shape #829, 8¼", $100.00 – 125.00.

Bottom row, from left:
Shape #27, 6", $40.00 – 50.00;
Shape #27, 6", $40.00 – 50.00;
Shape #D18 (three pieces), 2¾",
$10.00 – 15.00.

Shape #B7, lamp base, 11", $150.00 – 175.00.

Top row, from left:
Shape #795, 8¼", $95.00 – 125.00;
Shape #BA-1, 3" x 6½" dia., $30.00 – 40.00;
Shape #577, 5½", $30.00 – 40.00;
Shape #4, 7½", $55.00 – 75.00.

Bottom row, from left:
Shape #824, 9", $100.00 – 135.00;
Shape #515, 9", $125.00 – 150.00;
Shape #835, 7", $75.00 – 95.00.

Top row, from left:
Shape #BA-1, 6" dia., $30.00 – 40.00;
Shape #799, 7", $125.00 – 150.00;
Shape #BA-10, 6" dia., $40.00 – 60.00.

Bottom row, from left:
Shape #2VH, 12", $150.00 – 175.00;
Shape #827, 6", $65.00 – 95.00;
Shape #B7, 11", $100.00 – 125.00.

Top row, from left:
Shape #18, 2½", $20.00 – 30.00;
Shape #792, 8", $95.00 – 125.00;
Shape #792, 6", $65.00 – 95.00;
Shape #18, 2½", $20.00 – 30.00.

Bottom row, from left:
Shape #576, 8½", $65.00 – 85.00;
Shape #785, 8½", $75.00 – 95.00;
Shape #515, 9", $125.00 – 150.00.

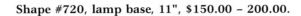

Shape #720, lamp base, 11", $150.00 – 200.00.

Top row, from left: Shape #513, 5", $45.00 – 55.00; Shape #835, 7", $65.00 – 95.00; Shape #830, 8½", $100.00 – 125.00. Bottom row, from left: Shape #B-7, 11", $100.00 – 125.00; Shape #864, 5" x 13½", $100.00 – 125.00.

From left: Shape #301, 12", $150.00 – 175.00; Shape #336, 7½", $50.00 – 60.00;
Shape #0, 5", $45.00 – 55.00.

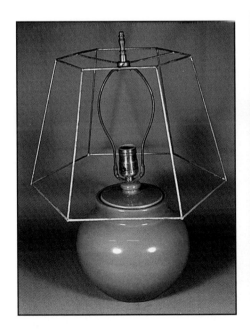

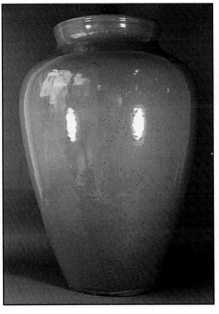

Shape #735, 8", $150.00 – 175.00.   Shape #108, 15", $150.00 – 250.00.   Shape #J, 12", $125.00 – 150.00.

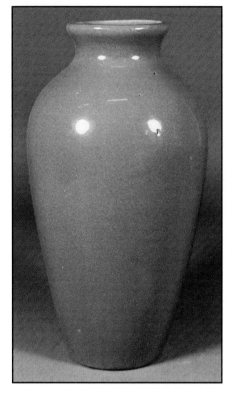

Shape #D23, 8", $75.00 – 115.00.

Shape #78, Old Pot Shop, 4" x 6", $45.00 – 50.00.

Left to right:
Shape #F4, heart, 4", $30.00 – 40.00;
Shape #B5, 9½", $125.00 – 150.00.

Shape #Old Pot Shop, 2½" dia., $40.00 – 55.00.

Shape #93, 6" dia., $35.00 – 50.00.

Shape #102, 8", $100.00 – 125.00.

Shape #551, 24", $450.00 – 650.00.

Top row, from left: Shape #F1, 4", $45.00 – 55.00; Shape #7, 12", $95.00 – 125.00; Shape #37, 11½", $125.00 – 150.00; Shape #301, 12", $150.00 – 175.00. Bottom row, from left: Shape #509, 4", $35.00 – 45.00; Shape #19, 9" dia., $65.00 – 95.00; Shape #5, 5½" dia., $35.00 – 45.00; Shape #102, 8", $125.00 – 150.00; Shape #D15, 5½", $65.00 – 95.00; Shape #564, 8½", $150.00 – 200.00; Shape #401, 2¾", $15.00 – 20.00; Shape #734, 6½", $45.00 – 55.00.

Shape #B17, 7", $75.00 – 95.00.

Shape #569, 11", $175.00 – 225.00.

Shape #564, 8½", $150.00 – 200.00.

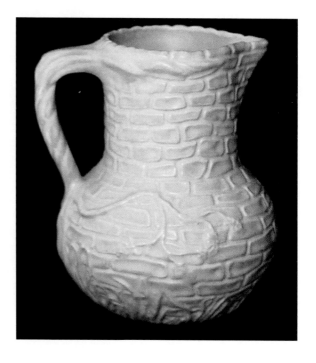

From left:
Shape #565,11", $150.00 – 200.00;
Shape #569, 11", $175.00 – 225.00;
Shape #564, 8", $150.00 – 200.00.

Shape #567, 7½", $150.00 – 175.00.   Shape #572, 2½" x 8¼" dia., $100.00 – 125.00.

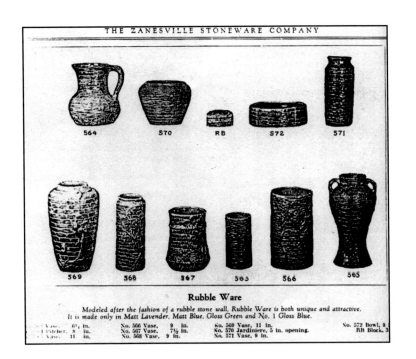

THE ZANESVILLE STONEWARE COMPANY

564   570   R B   572   571

569   568   567   565   566   565

Rubble Ware

Modeled after the fashion of a rubble stone wall, Rubble Ware is both unique and attractive.
It is made only in Matt Lavender, Matt Blue, Gloss Green and No. 1 Gloss Blue.

... Vase, 6½ in.	No. 566 Vase, 9 in.	No. 569 Vase, 11 in.	No. 572 Bowl, 8
... Pitcher, 8 in.	No. 567 Vase, 7½ in.	No. 570 Jardiniere, 5 in. opening.	RB Block, 3
... Vase, 11 in.	No. 568 Vase, 9 in.	No. 571 Vase, 9 in.	

**Shape #569, 11", lamp, $225.00 –
300.00.**

89

Shape #F28, 4", $95.00 – 125.00.

Shape not marked, 7¼" tall with the top in place. The body is 5¼"; the top is 2¾". Malcolm's House and Garden Store, Baltimore, Md., Frederick, Md., ink stamp, $150.00 – 200.00.

Shape #569, 11", lamp with cast base and top, $250.00 – 325.00.

From left:
Shape #766, 8", $325.00 – 425.00;
Shape #776, 7¾", $425.00 – 525.00.

Illustration of the Master Potter done by the French illustrator Edmund DuLac.

Verse XXXV
Rubaiyat of Omar Khayyam

Then to the Lip of this poor earthen Urn
I lean'd, the secret Well of Life to learn:
And Lip to Lip it murmur'd – "While you live,
Drink! – for once dead, you never shall return."

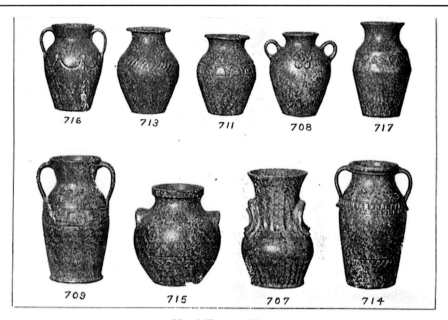

Hand-Thrown Ware

The charm of these lovely hand-thrown shapes is enhanced by the hand-marking and hand-finishing.
The finish is a neutral grayish-buff mottled effect like that of the large Oil Jars on Page 20.

No. 707 Vase, 11½ in.	per doz. $96.00	No. 711 Vase, 8½ in.	per doz. $48.00	No. 715 Vase, 10 in.	per doz. $96.00
No. 708 Vase, 9 in.	per doz. 60.00	No. 713 Vase, 9 in.	per doz. 48.00	No. 716 Vase, 9 in.	per doz. 60.00
No. 709 Vase, 12½ in.	per doz. 84.00	No. 714 Vase, 12½ in.	per doz. 72.00	No. 717 Vase, 10 in.	per doz. 60.00

Omar Ware

"Then to the lip of this poor earthen urn
I lean'd, the secret of my life to learn."

Omar Ware is more than a reproduction of ancient pottery; it is a continuation in the present of
the art of the past. The wet clay is thumped and batted, the shape is moulded by hand as the wheel
turns, in the same manner as that which inspired poets centuries ago. These old shapes, splashed with
a dash of color here and there on a dull buff back-ground, preserve the tradition of the potter's art.

765 Vase, 10¼ in.	each $9.00	No. 769 Vase, 10 in.	each $6.00	No. 773 Vase, 10¾ in.	each $10.00
766 Vase, 8 in.	each 5.00	No. 770 Vase, 8½ in.	each 5.00	No. 774 Vase, 9 in.	each 8.00
767 Vase, 8½ in.	each 6.00	No. 771 Vase, 10 in.	each 7.00	No. 775 Vase, 8 in.	each 11.00
768 Vase, 10½ in.	each 7.00	No. 772 Vase, 10¼ in.	each 9.00	No. 776 Vase, 7¾ in.	each 5.00

Catalog #10, page 8.

92

Shape #713, 9", $250.00 – 300.00.

Shape #715, 10", $300.00 – 375.00.

Shape #711, 8½", $275.00 – 375.00.

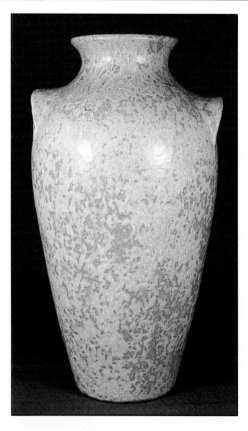

Above and below: unnumbered lamp base, 16", $325.00 – 400.00.

Shape #834, 7", $150.00 – 175.00.

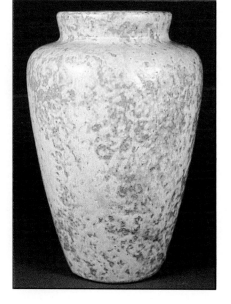

Shape #102, 8", $175.00 – 225.00.

Shape #23, 9", $175.00 – 225.00.

From left: Shape #851, 8", $50.00 – 75.00; Shape #37,12", $150.00 – 175.00.

Shape #J, 12", $175.00 – 250.00.

From left: Shape #B41, 6" dia., $40.00 – 70.00; Shape #791, 7", $125.00 – 150.00.

Shape #38, 10", $150.00 – 200.00.

Shape #J, 12", $200.00 – 250.00.

From left:
Shape #827, 6", $85.00 – 125.00;
Shape #38, 10", $150.00 – 200.00.

Shape #792, 8", $145.00 – 165.00.

From left:
Shape #827, 6", $85.00 – 125.00;
Shape #795, 8½", $150.00 – 175.00.

Shape #F2, 4" dia., $45.00 – 55.00.

From left: Shape #792, 8", $125.00 – 150.00; Shape not marked, 3", $75.00 – 100.00.

From left: Shape #800, 8", $125.00 – 150.00; Shape #795, 8½", $135.00 – 165.00.

Shape not marked, lamp base, 10",
$150.00 – 175.00.

Shape #833, 6¾", $75.00 – 100.00.

Shape #102, 8", $135.00 – 165.00.

Top row, from left: Shape #790, 16" x 16" dia., $400.00 – 600.00; Shape #B24, 18" x 12" dia., $550.00 – 750.00. Bottom row, from left: Shape not marked, lamp base, 7", $75.00 – 105.00; Shape #867, 6", $65.00 – 95.00; Shape #F4, heart 4", $45.00 – 55.00; Shape #J, 11½", $175.00 – 250.00; Shape #F1, 4", $45.00 – 55.00; Shape #J, 11½", $175.00 – 225.00.

From left:
Shape #792, 8", $125.00 – 150.00;
Shape #102, 8½", $135.00 – 165.00;
Shape #792, 8", $125.00 – 150.00.

Top row, from left: Shape #795, 8¾", $135.00 – 165.00; Shape #558, 15" x 15" dia., $450.00 – 650.00; Shape not marked, 8½" x 8½" dia., $175.00 – 225.00. Bottom row, from left: Shape #25, 7½" x 8½" dia., $150.00 – 200.00; Shape #102, 8½", $135.00 – 165.00; Shape #792, 8", $125.00 – 150.00; Shape #792, 8", $125.00 – 150.00.

Shape #38, 10", $150.00 – 200.00.

Top row, from left: Shape #12, 6", $65.00 – 75.00; Shape #18, 5" dia., $95.00 – 105.00; Shape #8, 6½", $100.00 – 125.00; Shape #9, 6", $100.00 – 125.00; Shape #20, 3¾"; $65.00 – 75.00. Bottom row, from left: Shape #66, 7" dia., $50.00 – 60.00; Shape #91, 6" dia., $75.00 – 100.00; Shape #78, 6" dia., $40.00 – 50.00.

From left:
Shape #8, 6½", $100.00 – 125.00;
Shape #20, 3¾", $65.00 – 75.00.

Vases, Bowls and Insets

A-1 Bowl,
4 in. ....per doz. $ 2.80
5 in. ....per doz. 4.00
6 in. ....per doz. 4.80

C Crown Holder,
2½ in. ....per doz. 3.60
3½ in. ....per doz. 6.00
4 in. ....per doz. 9.00
5 in. ....per doz. 12.00

D-23 Vase, 8 in., per doz. 9.00

E-1 Bowl, 5 in., per doz. 3.60

F Frog, 1½, per doz. 8.00

L Rustic Log, 3¾ in., per doz. $6.00

LP Lily Pad, 3¾ in., per doz. 8.00

P Block Holder,
2½ in. ....per doz. 3.60
3½ in. ....per doz. 4.80
5½ in. ....per doz. 7.20

T Turtle Holder ....per doz. 6.00

No. 6 Vase, 3 x 1½ in. per doz. 3.36

No. 26 Vase, 6 in. ....per doz. 6.00

No. 27 Vase, 6 in. ....per doz. $6.00

No. 32 Vase, 5 in., per doz. $ 6.00

No. 19 Wall Vase,
7 in. ....per doz. 6.00
9 in. ....per doz. 9.00
11 in. ....per doz. 12.00

No. 78 Flower Bowl,
3 in. ....per doz. $ 3.00
4 in. ....per doz. 3.50
5 in. ....per doz. 4.00
6 in. ....per doz. 6.00
8 in. ....per doz. 10.00
10 in. ....per doz. 16.00

No. 81 Bowl,
3 in. ....per doz. $ 3.00
5 in. ....per doz. 5.00

No. 85 Vase,
7 in. ....per doz. 6.00
10 in. ....per doz. 12.00

No. 87 Vase,
8 in. ....per doz. 6.00
12 in. ....per doz. 12.00

No. 91 Bowl, 6 in., per doz. 6.00
No. 92 Bowl, 5 in., per doz. 6.00
No. 93 Bowl, 6 in., per doz. 6.00
No. 94 Bowl, 5 in., per doz. 3.60
No. 95 Bowl, 6 in., per doz. 6.00

Colors: Assorted Matt and Gloss

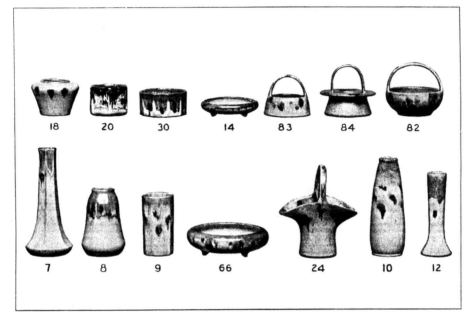

Zasko Ware [*Made with a gray glaze and dark blue runover.*]

No. 7 Vase, 11 in., per doz. $24.00
No. 8 Vase, 6½ in., per doz. 12.00
No. 9 Vase, 6 in., per doz. 6.00
No. 10 Vase, 10 in., per doz. 24.00
No. 12 Vase, 6 in., per doz. 6.00

No. 12 Vase, 7 in., per doz. $12.00
No. 12 Vase, 10 in., per doz. 18.00
No. 11 Bowl, 6 in., per doz. 6.00
No. 18 Bowl, 5 in., per doz. 6.00
No. 20 Bowl, 3¾ in., per doz. 6.00

No. 24 Basket 8 in. across,
9 in. tall ..per doz. $18.00
No. 30 Bowl, 5 in. ...per doz. 6.00
No. 30 Bowl, 6 in. ...per doz. 9.00
No. 66 Bowl, 7 in. ...per doz. 12.00

No. 66 Bowl, 8 in. ....per doz. $16.00
No. 66 Bowl, 9 in. ....per doz. 24.00
No. 82 Basket, 6 in. diam., per doz. 12.00
No. 83 Basket, 4 in. diam., per doz. 6.00
No. 84 Basket, 6 in. diam., per doz. 12.00

Clockwise from far left:
Shape #84, 6", $125.00 – 150.00;
Shape #66, 8", $65.00 – 75.00;
Shape #83, 4" dia., $100.00 – 125.00;
Shape #C, 3", $35.00 – 45.00;
Shape #83, 4" dia., $100.00 – 125.00.

From left:
Shape #18, 5", $95.00 – 105.00;
Shape #12, 6", $65.00 – 75.00;
Shape #8, 6½", $100.00 – 125.00.

Shape #82, 6", $125.00 – 150.00.

Shape #92, 5" dia., $95.00 – 105.00.

Shape not marked, 7½", $50.00 – 60.00.

From left: Shape #66, 7" dia., $50.00 – 60.00; Shape #66, 10" dia., $65.00 – 75.00.

From left: Shape #14, 6" dia., $50.00 – 60.00; Shape #78, 5" dia., $40.00 – 50.00;
Shape #95, 6" dia., $55.00 – 65.00.

From left: Shape #91, 5¾" dia., $75.00 – 100.00; Shape #30, 5" dia., $75.00 – 85.00; Shape #C1, 6¼" dia., $85.00 – 100.00.

Shape #9, 6", $100.00 – 125.00.   Shape #17, 6", $100.00 – 125.00.

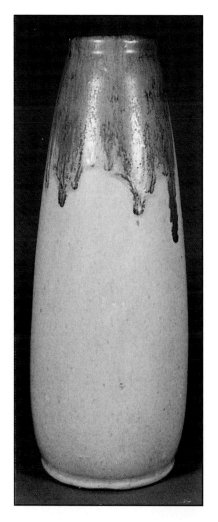 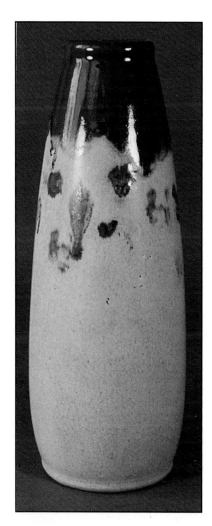

Shape #10, 10", two examples, $150.00 – 175.00 each.

Shape not marked, flower
block, 7" dia. x 1",
$45.00 – 75.00.

Verdantone

From left: Shape #102, 8", $150.00 – 175.00; Shape #38, 10", $200.00 – 250.00; Shape #795, 8½", $150.00 – 175.00.

Shape #86, 9", $125.00 – 145.00.

Top row: Shape not marked, 8¾" dia., $125.00 – 150.00. Bottom row, from left: Shape #10?, 6" dia., $100.00 – 125.00; Shape #RCB7, 6" dia., $75.00 – 100.00; Shape #51, 6¼" dia., $75.00 – 100.00.

From left: Shape not marked, 4½", $115.00 – 135.00; Shape #792, 6", $125.00 – 150.00.

From left: Shape #720, 9", $175.00 – 200.00; Shape #B3, 9", $200.00 – 225.00.

Shape #B21, 18", $450.00 – 650.00.

Shape #J, 12", $200.00 – 225.00.

Shape #B23, 25",
$700.00 – 1,000.00.

Shape #799, 7", $150.00 – 175.00.

From left: Shape #105, 7", $125.00 – 150.00; Shape #795, 8½", $150.00 – 175.00; Shape #102, 8", $150.00 – 175.00.

Shape #2VH, 12", $200.00 – 250.00.

From left: Shape #799, 7", $150.00 – 175.00; Shape #307, 8½", $175.00 – 200.00.

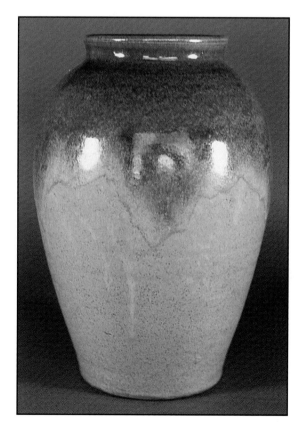

Shape #830, 8½", $125.00 – 150.00.

From left:
Shape #835, 7", $125.00 – 150.00;
Shape #839, 8", $135.00 – 165.00;
Shape #800, 8", $135.00 – 165.00.

Shape #795, 8½", $135.00 – 175.00.

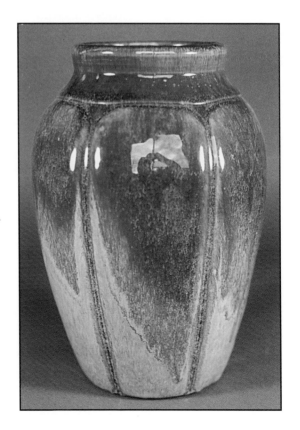

115

Shape #B22, 18", $450.00 – 650.00.

Shape #108, 22", $650.00 – 900.00.

Shape #B20, 18", $450.00 – 650.00.

Shape #847, 16½", $450.00 – 650.00.

Shape #F2, 4", $65.00 – 95.00.

Shape #B20, 18", $450.00 – 650.00.

Shape #4VH, 12", $175.00 – 225.00.

Shape #F2, 4", $65.00 – 75.00.

From left: Shape #827, 6", $95.00 – 125.00; Shape #B17, 6", $95.00 – 125.00.

Shape #101, 8½", $100.00 – 150.00.

From left:
Shape #F6, 4",
$65.00 – 95.00;
Shape #830, 8⅓",
$125.00 – 150.00.

119

Shape #838, 5¾", $125.00 – 150.00.

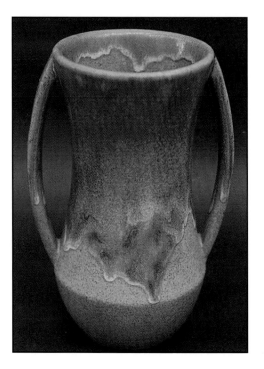

Shape #839, 8", $125.00 – 150.00.

From left:
Shape #834, 7", $125.00 – 150.00;
Shape #102, 8", $150.00 – 175.00.

Shape #108W, 15", $225.00 – 275.00.

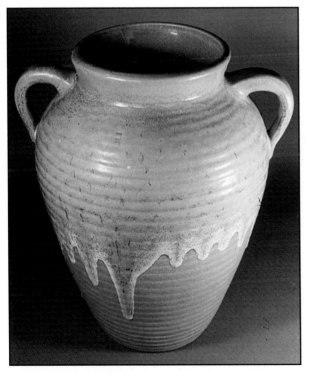

Shape #108 WH, 15", $250.00 – 300.00.

Shape #847, 16½", 3 applied handles, $300.00 – 350.00.

From left:
Shape #26, 7" dia., $75.00 – 100.00;
Shape not marked, 8¾", $95.00 – 115.00.

Variety Glazes, Shapes, and Novelties

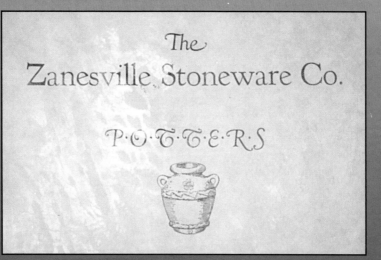

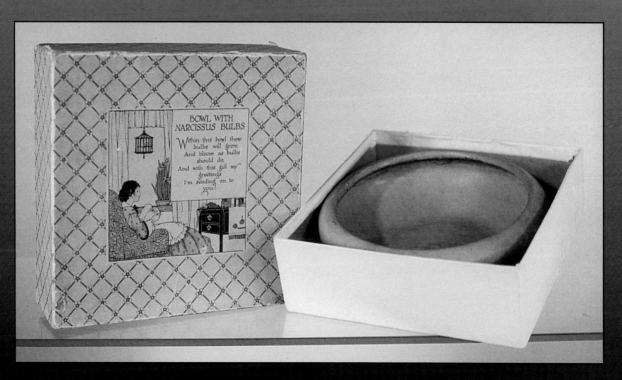

Gift box and bowl #78, $75.00 – 95.00.

Shape #102, 8", $125.00 – 175.00.

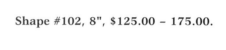

Shape #102, 8", $125.00 – 175.00.

Shape #102, 8", $125.00 – 175.00.

Shape #102, 8", glaze varieties,
$125.00 – 175.00 each.

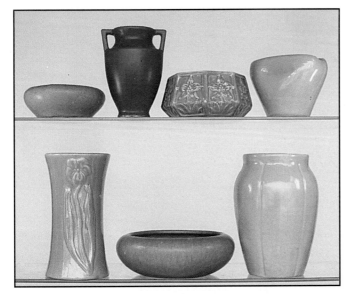

Top row, from left:
Shape #5, 6" dia., $20.00 – 40.00;
Shape #792, 6", $100.00 – 125.00;
Shape #BA-10, 3" x 6" dia., $40.00 – 60.00;
Shape #F-2, 4", $30.00 – 40.00.

Bottom row, from left:
Shape #576, 9", $75.00 – 95.00;
Shape #78, 8" dia., $40.00 – 50.00;
Shape #837, 9", $75.00 – 95.00.

Shape #108, 18", $150.00 – 200.00.

From left:
Shape #101, 8½", $125.00 – 150.00;
Shape #322, 6½", $65.00 – 95.00.

From left:
Shape #21, 10", $150.00 – 175.00;
Shape #21, 8", $125.00 – 150.00.

Top row, from left: Shape #D-6, 5", $30.00 – 40.00; Shape #D-3, 3½", $25.00 – 35.00; Shape #D-4, 5½", $40.00 – 50.00; Shape #D-6, 5", $30.00 – 40.00. Bottom row, from left: Shape #822, 5", $75.00 – 100.00; Shape #511, 4", $45.00 – 55.00; Shape #D-13, 5", $65.00 – 95.00.

Top row, from left:
Shape, Dutchess Cheese, 3", $25.00 – 35.00;
Shape #730, 8", $125.00 – 150.00;
Shape #735, 7", $125.00 – 150.00.

Center row:
Shape, Wally Frank Ltd., 4", $75.00 – 100.00.

Bottom row, from left:
Shape, Dutchess Cheese bottom, $20.00 – 25.00;
3 Shapes, Dutchess Cheese, 3", $25.00 – 35.00;
Shape not marked, 5", $75.00 – 100.00.

Shape #515X, 5" mugs, $30.00 – 40.00.

From left: Shape #D18, 3" dia., $30.00 – 40.00; Shape #D18, Old Pot Shop, 4" dia., $50.00 – 60.00; Shape #D18, Old Pot Shop, 5" dia., $65.00 – 75.00.

Shape #81, 2" x 3" dia., $35.00 – 45.00.

Shape #B9, 10", $150.00 – 175.00.

Shape #B4, 11", $150.00 – 175.00.

Shape #B9, 10", $150.00 – 200.00.

Shape #580, 4¼" tumblers, $20.00 – 30.00.

Shape #579, 8¾" pitchers, $125.00 – 150.00.

Shape not marked, 3½",
$50.00 – 60.00.

From left:
Shape not marked, 5" dia., $35.00 – 45.00;
Shape #B1, 5" dia., $25.00 – 35.00.

From left: Shape #522, 9", $125.00 – 150.00; Shape #524, 9", $125.00 – 150.00; Shape #522, 9", $125.00 – 150.00.

Shape #795, 8½" vase, assorted colors, $100.00 – 125.00.

Shape #1V, 12" x 8" dia., $150.00 – 200.00.

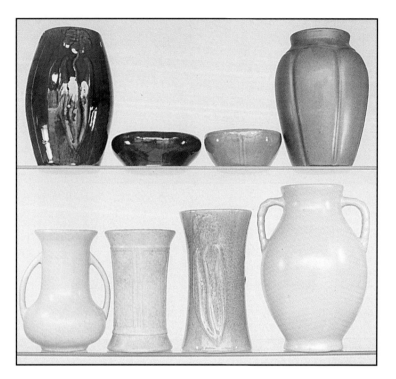

Top row, from left:
Shape #101, 8½", $75.00 – 100.00;
Shape #5, 2" x 6" dia., $25.00 – 35.00;
Shape #B2, 2" x 5" dia., $25.00 – 35.00;
Shape #795, 8½", $125.00 – 150.00;

Bottom row, from left:
Shape #835, 7", $100.00 – 125.00;
Shape #834, 7", $100.00 – 125.00;
Shape #576, 8½", $75.00 – 100.00;
Shape #338, 10", $125.00 – 150.00.

From left: Shape #B2, 5" dia., $25.00 – 35.00; Shape #B1, 5" dia., $25.00 – 35.00; Shape #94, 5" dia., $25.00 – 35.00; Shape #B2, 5" dia., $25.00 – 35.00.

Shape #792, 6", clear gloss, $100.00 – 125.00.

Shape not marked, Old Pot Shop, 4", clear gloss,
$115.00 – 145.00.

Shape #795, 8½", $125.00 – 150.00.

From left: Shape, Cup #575, 3½" dia., $25.00 – 35.00; Shape,
Saucers #575, 5¾" dia., $15.00 – 20.00; Shape, Plate #574, 8½"
dia., $40.00 – 50.00.

Shape #2VH, 12", $250.00 – 300.00.

Shape #847, 16½", $350.00 – 550.00.

Shape #838, 5¾", $125.00 – 150.00.

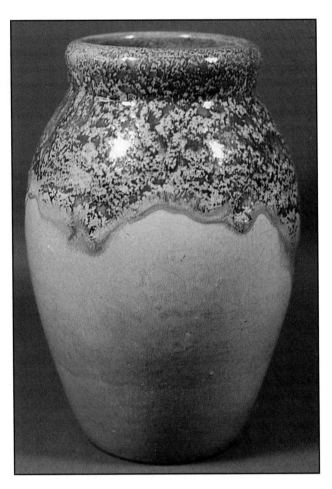

Shape #J, 12", $175.00 – 225.00.

Shape #J, 12", Bacorcy black flow over light green, $175.00 – 225.00.

Shape #B20, 16", $550.00 – 750.00.

Shape #B20, 16", $400.00 – 550.00.

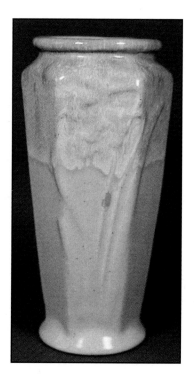

Top row, from left: Shape #835, 7", $100.00 – 125.00; Shape #792, 8", $100.00 – 125.00; Shape not marked, 3", $75.00 – 100.00; Shape #839, 8", $125.00 – 145.00. Bottom row, from left: Shape #38, 10", $150.00 – 200.00; Shape #795, 8½", $150.00 – 175.00; Shape #795, 8½", $125.00 – 150.00.

Shape #824, 9", $125.00 – 150.00.

Shape #87, 6¼" dia. bowls, $40.00 – 50.00 each.

Shape #N/M, Old Pot Shop, 3½" x 5½" dia., $40.00 – 50.00.

Shape #101, 8½", $150.00 – 175.00.

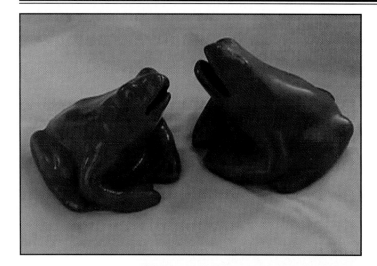

Frog shape #801, 5", $75.00 – 105.00.

From left:
Shape #316, 6¼",
$75.00 – 105.00;
Shape #316, 9",
$125.00 – 150.00.

From left:
Shape #314, 5⅛", $65.00 – 95.00;
Shape #316, 6¼", $75.00 – 100.00.

Shape #F26, 7½", $60.00 – 95.00.

From left: Shape #BA12, 6", $45.00 – 55.00; Shape #BA13, 5¼", $25.00 – 45.00; Shape #BA14, 5½", $45.00 – 55.00.

Shape #722, 5½", gazing globe base, $150.00 – 200.00.

Shape #713, 8", $200.00 – 250.00.

From left:
Shape #51, lamp base, 8",
$125.00 – 150.00;
Shape not marked, 8½",
$100.00 – 125.00;
Shape not marked, 11¼",
$125.00 – 150.00;
Shape #51, lamp base, 8",
$125.00 – 150.00.

Lamp base bottoms.

Shape not marked. 7" h, 16" d, 10" h with top, atomizer, insert marked Walton Atomizing Unit Series IFP, $100.00 – 150.00.

Shape not marked, 6", $15.00 – 25.00.

Shape not marked, 5½", $15.00 – 25.00.

143

Shape not marked, 6", 3", 6", $15.00 – 25.00.

Rosemary Cologne perfume decanters, labeled,
$35.00 – 45.00 each.

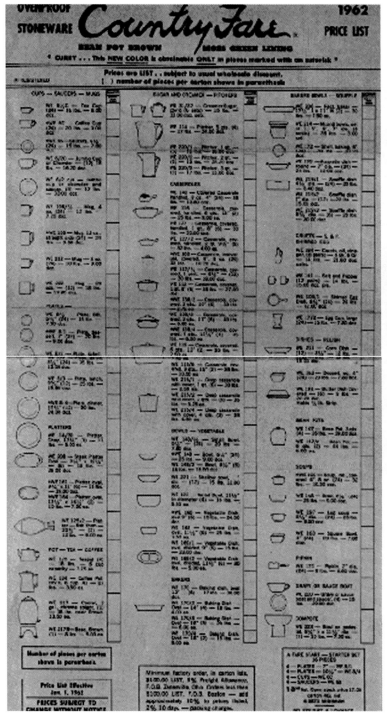

Casseroles with lids, $35.00 – 75.00 each.

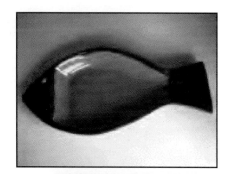

Clockwise, from left: Mug set, shape #WE 106, 5", $15.00 – 25.00; condiment set, shape #WE 141, which includes salt and pepper, #WE 184, $10.00 – 15.00; cruet, not marked, $15.00 – 25.00, and covered sugar, $10.00 – 20.00; one-handled casserole dish, shape #WE 116, $20.00 – 35.00; cruets, shape #WE 184, $15.00 – 25.00; relish tray, shape #N/M, 15", $60.00 – 70.00.

The

ZANESVILLE STONEWARE COMPANY

Zanesville, Ohio

Manufacturers of

Plain and Decorated Stoneware

Water Filters, Coolers, Garden Pots, Florists Vases, Toilet, Kitchen Specialties, Etc.

Catalogue Number 4

1912

OUR terms are F. O. B. Zanesville, Ohio. 30 days net or 2 per cent. discount for cash in ten days.

We make no charge for packing or packages.

Stoneware Counts as Follows:

$1/8$ gallon ware counts $2/5$ gallon.
$1/4$ gallon ware counts $1/2$ gallon.
$1/2$ gallon ware counts $2/3$ gallon.
$3/4$ gallon ware counts $7/8$ gallon.

COVERS FOR BUTTER JARS COUNT:

Under 1 gallon same as vessel for which intended.
Covers for 1 and 2 gallons count 1 gallon each.
Covers for 3 and 4 gallons count $1\frac{1}{2}$ gallons each.
Covers for 5 and 6 gallons count 2 gallons each.
Covers for 8, 10, 12 gallons count 3 gallons each.
Covers for 16 and 20 gallons count 4 gallons each.
Covers for 25 and 30 gallons count 6 gallons each.

COVERS FOR PRESERVE JARS COUNT:

For 2 gallons and under, $1/3$ gallon each.
For 3 gallons and over, $2/3$ gallons each.

Catalog #4.

THE ZANESVILLE STONEWARE CO.

ZANESVILLE, OHIO.

STONE WATER FILTER

We at all times carry a large stock of the goods shown herein and can fill orders promptly. Our goods present an attractive appearance coupled with an unequalled quality for serviceableness, and command a growing demand wherever introduced. We defy competition, quality considered, and have a line of staples that are always in demand.

We respectfully solicit your patronage and assure you of complete satisfaction.

The process of filtering is shown in the cut, by percolation through a porous natural stone from the upper to the lower jar simply by the force of gravity, which is nature's own process of filtering.

The Absolute Essentials of a Good Filter are:

1st.—Simplicity in construction.

2nd.—That every part of the Filter shall be easily gotten at for the purpose of cleansing.

3rd.—That the medium be an efficient purifier and permit the water to pass slowly, otherwise it is only an attempt at filtering.

4th.—That the Purifying medium shall not receive into its pores the filth it extracts.

5th.—That the whole construction of the Filter shall be lasting.

6th.—That metal must not be used in the construction of the Filter, as it is always bad and nearly always poisonous, and imparts an unpleasant taste to the water.

All these conditions are met in the Zanesville Stone Water Filter.

2

3

Catalog #4.

THE ZANESVILLE STONEWARE CO.

ZANESVILLE, OHIO.

CUT SHOWING COMPARATIVE SIZES
OF FILTERS.

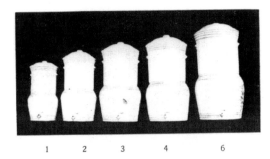

1   2   3   4   6

No. 1. Capacity per day, 2 to 3 gallons. Diameter filtering disc, 7 inches. Upper jar holds 5 quarts, lower jar 7 quarts. Each....................................

No. 2.—Capacity per day, 3 to 5 gallons. Diameter filtering disc, 8¼ inches. Upper jar holds 9 quarts, lower jar 12 quarts. Each.........................

No. 3. Capacity per day, 4 to 8 gallons. Diameter filtering disc, 9 inches. Upper jar holds 12 quarts, lower jar 17 quarts. Each....................

No. 4. Capacity per day, 6 to 10 gallons. Diameter filtering disc, 10 inches. Upper jar holds 16 quarts, lower jar 21 quarts. Each....................

No. 6. Capacity per day, 10 to 14 gallons. Diameter filtering disc, 11 inches. Upper jar holds 24 quarts, lower jar 30 quarts. Each................

————

We can furnish these filters in either blue mottled finish, or plain with blue bands as may be preferred. Also with a turn key or self closing faucet at option of the buyer, but in absence of instructions we fill orders with the blue mottled finish and turn key faucet.

WATER COOLERS, KEG SHAPE.
White With Blue Bands
2, 3, 4 and 6 Gal. Sizes.

WATER COOLERS STRAIGHT, JAR SHAPE.
Blue Mottled, or White With Blue Bands
2, 3, 4, 5, 6, 8, 10 and 12 Gal Sizes.

————

Both styles are complete with cover and large size nickle plated brass faucet, either self closing or turn key as may be preferred.

4

5

Catalog #4.

THE ZANESVILLE STONEWARE CO.

ZANESVILLE, OHIO.

ITALIAN FLOWER POTS AND SAUCERS

9 inch
13 inch
16 inch
21 inch

These are a most stylish pot for formal gardens, steps, porches, etc., and appeal to the best class of trade.

Made in Green Matt Glaze.
We can also furnish them in a light cream colored glaze.

UMBRELLA JAR
No. 1
10x21 inch
Green Matt Glaze

JARDINIER
No. 600
8 inch
10 inch
Green Matt Glaze.

6

Catalog #4.

THE ZANESVILLE STONEWARE CO.   ZANESVILLE, OHIO.

JARDINER NO. 601

5, 6, 7, 8 and 10 inch
Green Matt Glaze

UMBRELLA JAR
No. 2

10x21 inch

Green Matt Glaze

FLORISTS VASES FOR CUT FLOWERS

Sizes

3	x 4½ in.	5½ x 10 in.
4	x 6 in.	4 x 12 in.
3	x 9 in.	4½ x 15 in.
4½ x 9 in.		5½ x 18 in.

Inside measurements.

Green Matt Glaze.

JARDINER NO. 0

4 inch	7 inch
5 inch	8 inch
6 inch	10 inch

Green Matt Glaze

8   9

Catalog #4.

THE ZANESVILLE STONEWARE CO.

ZANESVILLE, OHIO.

CEMETERY VASE
(Without hole—like cut)

WALL VASE
(With hole for hanging)

In ordering state which is wanted.

FERN DISH AND LINER
7 inch
9 inch

Our Green Matt is a hard fired, hard bodied ware that will hold water and will stand exposure to the weather without deterioration. It is strong and durable as the hills and a color that harmonizes with any and all surroundings.

Give us an order for a trial lot. No charge for crating, F. O. B. Zanesville, O.

HALL BOY JUGS
3½ Pints

Made in assorted colors, Brown, Blue and Green outside. White lined.

OCTAGON JUG
2 Qt.

Made in Mahogany Glaze outside. White lined, and in blue stipple.

10

11

Catalog #4.

THE ZANESVILLE STONEWARE CO.   ZANESVILLE, OHIO.

GROWLER
5 and 7 pint

Made in Mahogany outside.   White lined, and also in blue stipple.

COVERED BUTTERS
Made white with blue bands, blue stippled and Mahogany. White lined.

2, 3 and 5 lb.

SHOP OR MECHANICS' PITCHER
(Heavy Stone. White Glazed.)

2 quarts   6 quarts
4 quarts   8 quarts

COVERED SALT BOX
6 inch

Made blue stippled, Mahogany, white lined, or white with blue bands.

BEER MUGS
(12 ounce)

Made plain with blue bands or Mahogany. White lined.

HIGH BACK SALT BOX
(Blue Bands)

12   13

Catalog #4.

THE ZANESVILLE STONEWARE CO.   ZANESVILLE, OHIO.

MIXING BOWLS

7½ inches	10½ inches
8½ inches	11½ inches
9½ inches	12½ inches

TEA POTS
(Mahogany, White Lined)

Individual
2 pints
3 pints

BAKERS

5 inch	8 inch
6 inch	9 inch
7 inch	10 inch

We make these Bowls and Bakers in Mahogany, white lined and in a two color "Agate" stipple.

BOSTON BEAN POTS

1 Qt.	4 Qt.
2 Qt.	6 Qt.
3 Qt.	

INDIVIDUAL BAKER
4 inch

CUSTARD CUPS
3¼ inch
3¾ inch
(Mahogany, White Lined)

INDIVIDUAL BEAN POTS
½ pint
1 pint
(Mahogany Glazed)

14   15

Catalog #4.

THE ZANESVILLE STONEWARE CO.   ZANESVILLE, OHIO.

PIPKINS
(Dark Glaze)

With covers and white lined.
1 pint, 1 quart, 2 quart, 3 quart and 4 quart.

EWERS AND BASINS

9s

Plain white and stippled.

CASSEROLES

6 inch
8 inch
10 inch
12 inch

(Mahogany, White Lined)

CHAMBERS

12s, 9s and 6s

Plain and stippled. Open and covered.

16   17

Catalog #4.

THE ZANESVILLE STONEWARE CO.

ZANESVILLE. OHIO.

COMBINETS

No. 3

Stippled and banded or plain.

No. 7

Plain or with stippled border.

TOILET SETS

12 piece. See cut.

10 piece. Same, less covered jar.

7 piece. E. and B., covered jar, covered chamber and soap slab.

5 piece. E. and B., covered chamber and soap slab.

18

19

Catalog #4.

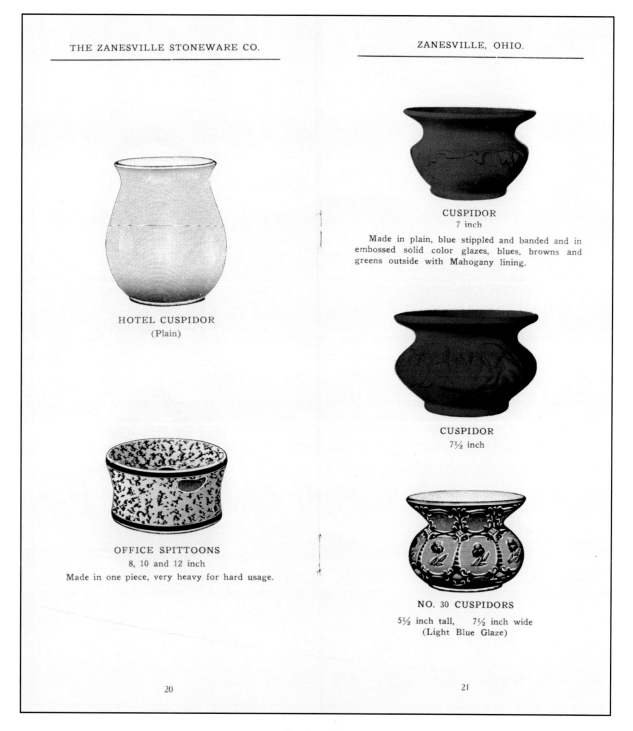

THE ZANESVILLE STONEWARE CO.

ZANESVILLE, OHIO.

CUSPIDOR
7 inch

Made in plain, blue stippled and banded and in embossed solid color glazes, blues, browns and greens outside with Mahogany lining.

HOTEL CUSPIDOR
(Plain)

CUSPIDOR
7½ inch

OFFICE SPITTOONS
8, 10 and 12 inch
Made in one piece, very heavy for hard usage.

NO. 30 CUSPIDORS
5½ inch tall,   7½ inch wide
(Light Blue Glaze)

20

21

Catalog #4.

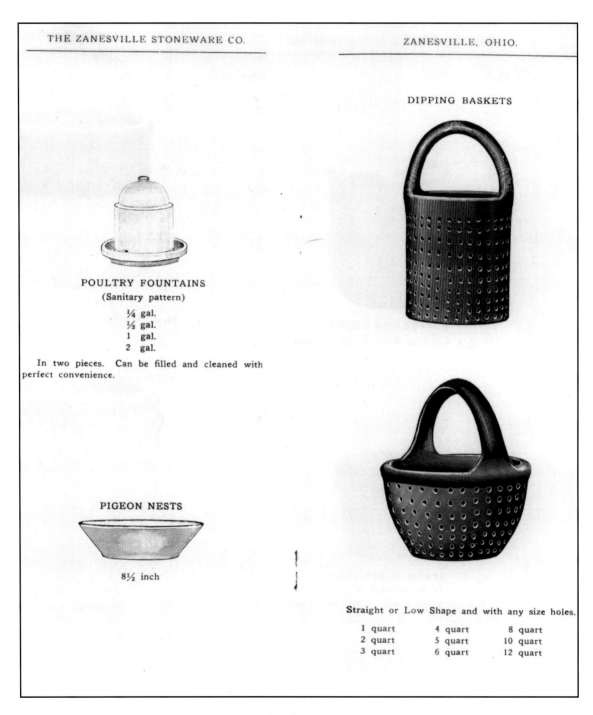

THE ZANESVILLE STONEWARE CO.   ZANESVILLE, OHIO.

DIPPING BASKETS

POULTRY FOUNTAINS
(Sanitary pattern)

¼ gal.
½ gal.
1 gal.
2 gal.

In two pieces. Can be filled and cleaned with
perfect convenience.

PIGEON NESTS

8½ inch

Straight or Low Shape and with any size holes.

1 quart	4 quart	8 quart
2 quart	5 quart	10 quart
3 quart	6 quart	12 quart

Catalog #4.

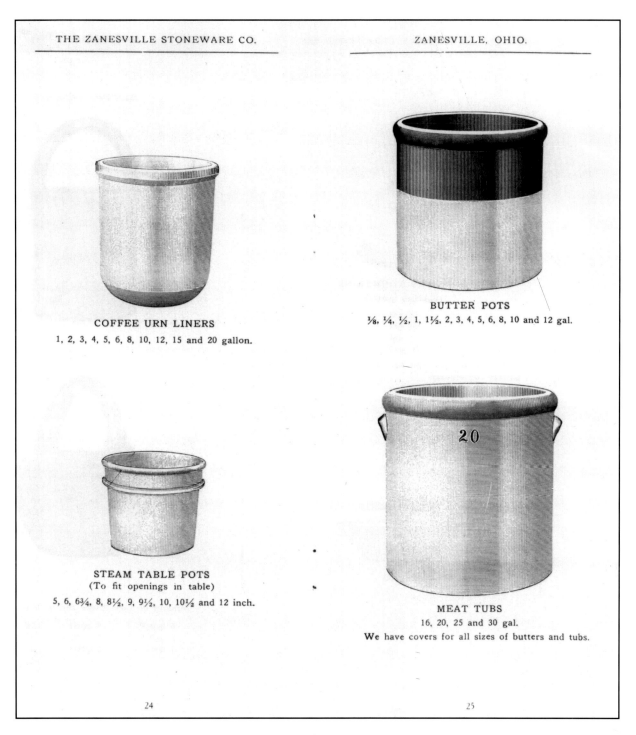

THE ZANESVILLE STONEWARE CO.

ZANESVILLE, OHIO.

COFFEE URN LINERS
1, 2, 3, 4, 5, 6, 8, 10, 12, 15 and 20 gallon.

BUTTER POTS
⅛, ¼, ½, 1, 1½, 2, 3, 4, 5, 6, 8, 10 and 12 gal.

STEAM TABLE POTS
(To fit openings in table)
5, 6, 6¾, 8, 8½, 9, 9½, 10, 10½ and 12 inch.

MEAT TUBS
16, 20, 25 and 30 gal.
We have covers for all sizes of butters and tubs.

24

25

Catalog #4.

159

THE ZANESVILLE STONEWARE CO.   ZANESVILLE, OHIO.

MILK PANS
(Round and Flat Bottom)
⅛, ¼, ½, ¾, 1, 1½ and 2 gal.
Both White and Black Glazed

FRENCH POTS
½, ¾, 1 and 1½ gal.
White Glazed

PRESERVE JAR
(With stone cover)
¼, ½, 1, 1½, 2, ,3, 4, 5
and 6 gal.
White and Black Glazed

CHURNS
1, 1½, 2, 3, 4, 5, 6, 8 and 10 gal.
Covers for 1 to 6 gal. count 1 gal.
Covers for 8 to 10 gal. count 2 gal.

LOW BUTTERS
⅛, ¼, ½, 1 and 2 gal.

BREAD BOWLS
(17 inch)
White Glazed

DRUGGISTS JUGS
(Either blue band or black top)
¼, ½ and 1 gal.

26   27

Catalog #4.

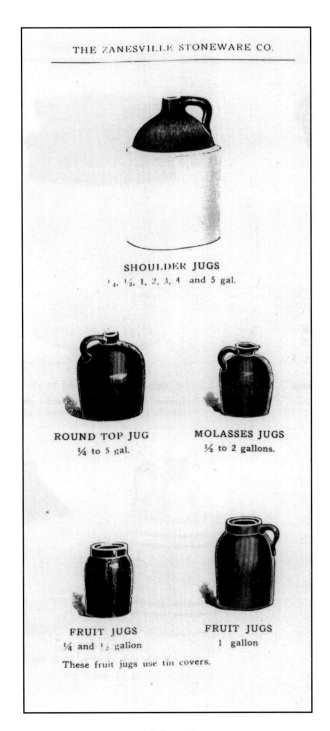

THE ZANESVILLE STONEWARE CO.

SHOULDER JUGS
¼, ½, 1, 2, 3, 4 and 5 gal.

ROUND TOP JUG
¼ to 5 gal.

MOLASSES JUGS
½ to 2 gallons.

FRUIT JUGS
¼ and ½ gallon

FRUIT JUGS
1 gallon

These fruit jugs use tin covers.

Catalog #4.

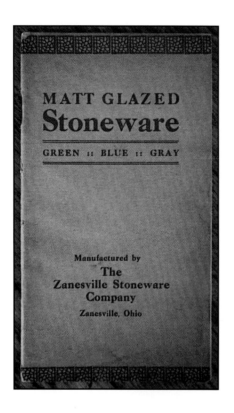

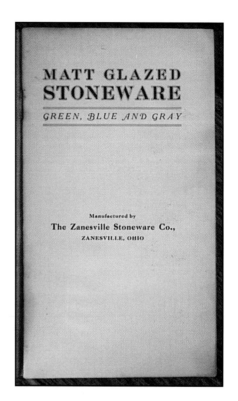

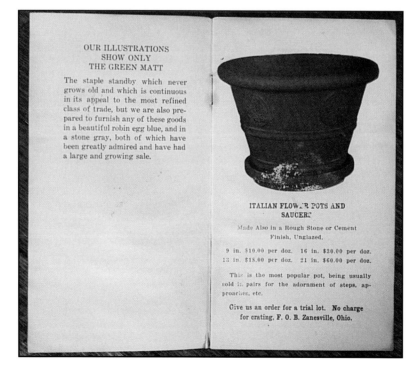

OUR ILLUSTRATIONS
SHOW ONLY
THE GREEN MATT

The staple standby which never grows old and which is continuous in its appeal to the most refined class of trade, but we are also prepared to furnish any of these goods in a beautiful robin egg blue, and in a stone gray, both of which have been greatly admired and have had a large and growing sale.

ITALIAN FLOWER POTS AND
SAUCERS

Made Also in a Rough Stone or Cement
Finish, Unglazed.

9 in. $10.00 per doz.   16 in. $30.00 per doz.
13 in. $18.00 per doz.   21 in. $60.00 per doz.

This is the most popular pot, being usually sold in pairs for the adornment of steps, approaches, etc.

Give us an order for a trial lot. No charge for crating, F. O. B. Zanesville, Ohio.

Catalog #5.

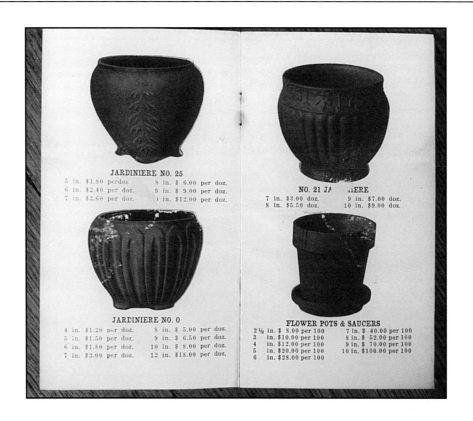

JARDINIERE NO. 25

5 in. $1.80 per doz	8 in. $ 6.00 per doz.
6 in. $2.40 per doz.	9 in. $ 9.00 per doz.
7 in. $3.60 per doz.	) in. $12.00 per doz.

NO. 21 JA   IERE

| 7 in. $3.00 doz. | 9 in. $7.00 doz. |
| 8 in. $5.50 doz. | 10 in. $9.00 doz. |

JARDINIERE NO. 0

4 in. $1.20 per doz.	8 in. $ 5.00 per doz.
5 in. $1.50 per doz.	9 in. $ 6.50 per doz.
6 in. $1.80 per doz.	10 in. $ 8.00 per doz.
7 in. $3.00 per doz.	12 in. $18.00 per doz.

FLOWER POTS & SAUCERS

2½ in. $ 8.00 per 100	7 in. $ 40.00 per 100
3 in. $10.00 per 100	8 in. $ 52.00 per 100
4 in. $12.00 per 100	9 in. $ 70.00 per 100
5 in. $20.00 per 100	10 in. $100.00 per 100
6 in. $28.00 per 100	

JAPANESE GARDEN BOWLS

9 in. $ 3.60 doz.	16 in. $20.00 doz.
11 in. $ 6.00 doz.	18 in. $36.00 doz.
13 in. $12.00 doz.	

JARDINIERE
No. 600

| 8 in. $ per doz. |
| 10 in. $12.00 per doz. |

TRUMPET CUT FLOWER VASES

| 12 in. $10.00 per d |
| 18 in. $20.00 per   . |
| 24 in. $40.00 per doz. |

'ANGING BASKET
With Chain and Liner
10¾ in. $10.00 doz.

Catalog #5.

163

UMBRELLA JAR
No. 1
10x21 in. $20.00 per doz.

UMBRELLA JAR
No. 2
10x21 in. $20.00 per doz.

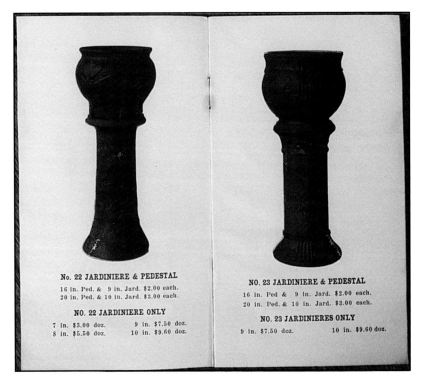

No. 22 JARDINIERE & PEDESTAL
16 in. Ped. & 9 in. Jard. $2.00 each.
20 in. Ped. & 10 in. Jard. $3.00 each.

NO. 22 JARDINIERE ONLY
7 in. $3.00 doz.   9 in. $7.50 doz.
8 in. $5.50 doz.   10 in. $9.60 doz.

NO. 23 JARDINIERE & PEDESTAL
16 in. Ped. & 9 in. Jard. $2.00 each.
20 in. Ped. & 10 in. Jard. $3.00 each.

NO. 23 JARDINIERES ONLY
9 in. $7.50 doz.   10 in. $9.60 doz.

Catalog #5.

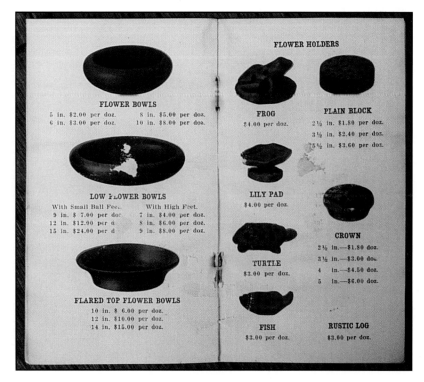

Catalog #5.

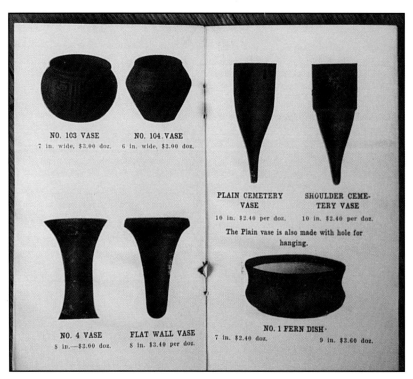

Catalog #5.

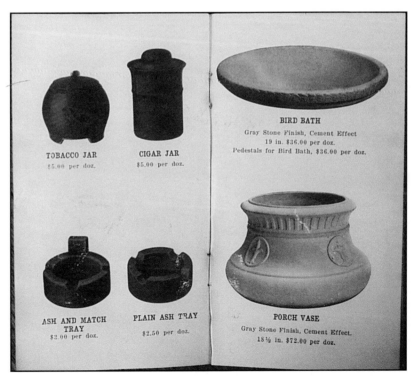

Catalog #5.

167

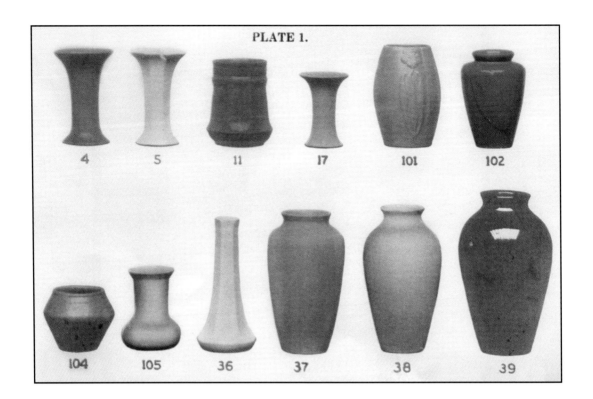

Catalog #7.

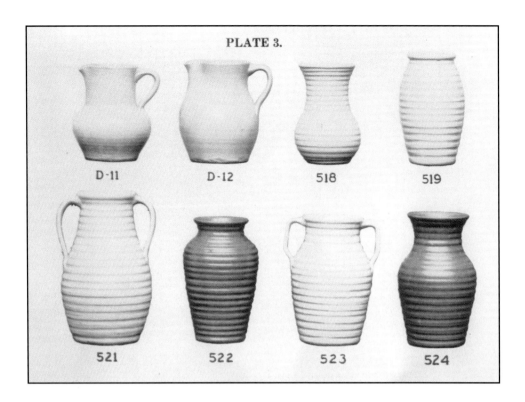

PLATE 3.

D-11   D-12   518   519

521   522   523   524

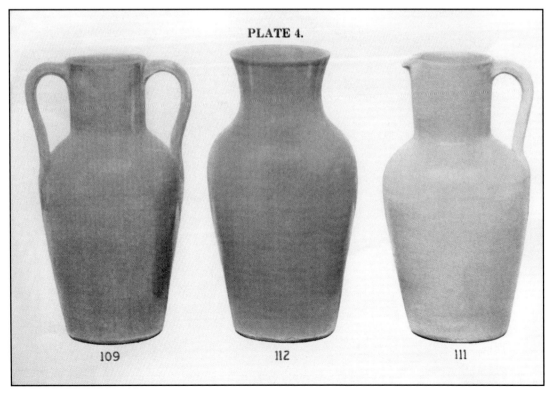

PLATE 4.

109   112   111

Catalog #7.

PLATE 5.

106   118   120

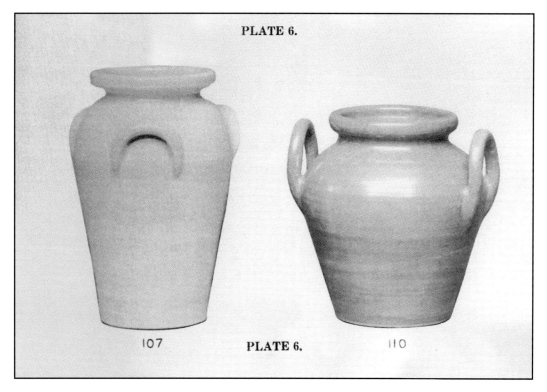

PLATE 6.

107   PLATE 6.   110

Catalog #7.

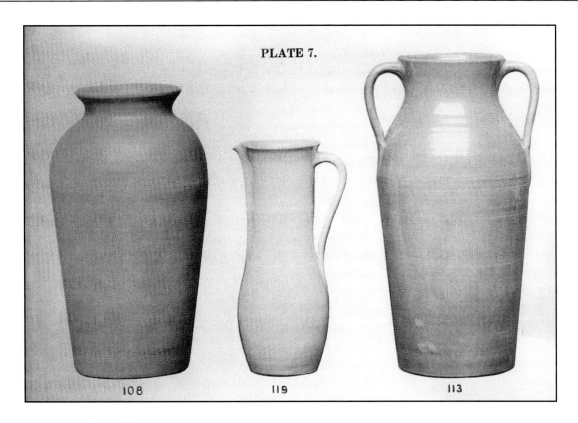

PLATE 7.

108   119   113

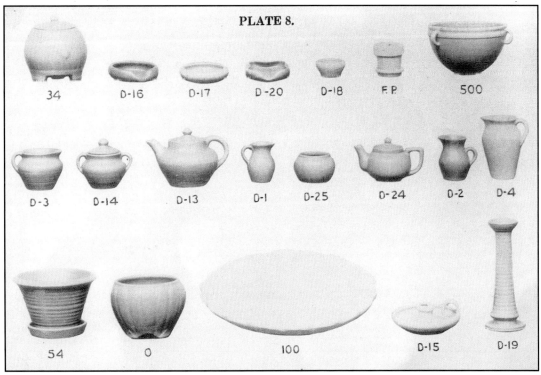

PLATE 8.

34   D-16   D-17   D-20   D-18   F.P.   500

D-3   D-14   D-13   D-1   D-25   D-24   D-2   D-4

54   0   100   D-15   D-19

Catalog #7.

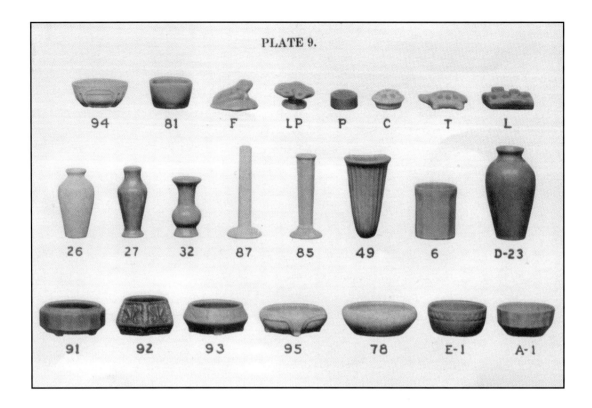

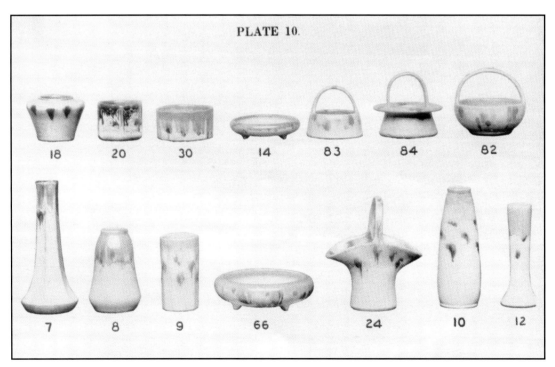

Catalog #7.

172

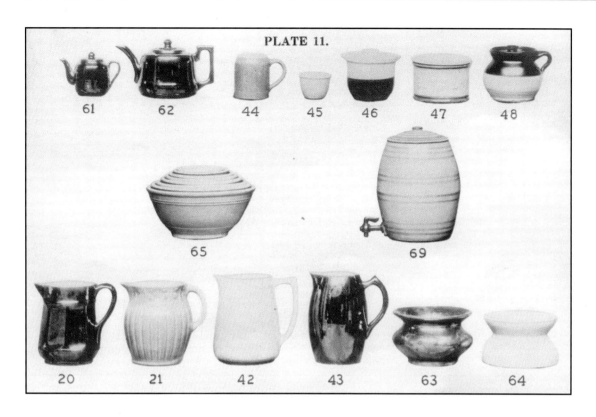

Catalog #7.

173

THE
ZANESVILLE STONEWARE COMPANY

Manufacturers of

ART WARE, GARDEN WARE
and HIGH-GRADE GLAZED
SPECIALTIES

Zanesville, Ohio, U. S. A.

THE ZANESVILLE STONEWARE COMPANY

FOREWORD

All the ware illustrated in this catalogue is made in a hard-fired body, colored in a variety of glazes, gloss and matt. Strength and durability are therefore added to pleasing appearance.

Colors.

Colors are Matt Green, Matt Rose, Matt Lavender, light and dark Matt Blue, Gloss Blue, Gloss Green, Gloss Rose, Gloss Lavender, Gloss Black, Zasko and Bristol White. Pages 4 to 9 of the catalogue, items which are produced almost exclusively in Matt Green, show that color only, but pages 10 and 11 show the different colors.

Matt Green is illustrated by Nos. 220, 102 and 101, Pages 10, 11.	Dark Matt Blue is illustrated by No. 4, Page 10.
Matt Rose is illustrated by Nos. 60 and 5, Page 10.	Gloss Blue is illustrated by No. 38, Page 11.
Matt Lavender is illustrated by Nos. 11 and 36, Pages 10 and 11.	Gloss Green is illustrated by No. 105, Page 11.
Light Matt Blue is illustrated by Nos. 104 and 37, Page 11.	Gloss Rose is illustrated by No. 103, Page 11.

Matt Green Ware.

Attention is called to the line of Matt Green Jardinieres, Flower Pots, and so forth, illustrated in the first several pages of the catalogue. Matt Green is the staple standby that never grows old and is continuous in its appeal to the most refined class of trade.

Hand-Thrown Ware.

Attention is likewise directed to our line of genuine hand-made ware, turned up on a potter's wheel. The slight deviations and irregularities left by the potter's hands give to each piece individuality and beauty.

Pottery for Porch, Lawn and Garden.

Pages 32 to 35 show our pottery for Porch, Lawn and Garden. It is made in a rough gray stone effect which is most attractive and accommodates itself to any surroundings.

Hotel, Kitchen, and Utility Ware.

Items of Hotel, Kitchen, and Utility Ware are illustrated on Page 37. The colors in which this class of ware is glazed are Gloss Blue, Gloss Green, Mahogany, and Brown and White. In quality of workmanship and design, we believe these specialties to be unexcelled by any similar line.

Catalog #9.

THE ZANESVILLE STONEWARE COMPANY

INDEX TO PAGES

Page 4—Italian Pot and Jardinieres and Pedestals.

Page 5—Jardinieres.

Page 6—Cut Flower Vases.

Page 7—Flower or Lamp Vases.

Page 8—Cemetery and Wall Vases, Flower Pot, Fern Dishes, Specialties.

Page 9—Umbrella or Sand Jars.

Page 10—Flower Vases.

Page 11—Flower Vases.

Page 12—Hand-thrown Ware.

Page 13—Hand-thrown Ware.

Page 14—Art and Gift Novelties, Hand-thrown Vases.

Page 15—Hand-thrown Ware.

Page 16—Large Hand-thrown Oil Jars.

Page 17—Large Hand-thrown Oil Jars.

Page 18—Large Hand-thrown Jars.

Page 19—Large Hand-thrown Jars.

Page 20—Large Hand-thrown Jars.

Page 21—Large Hand-thrown Jars.

Page 22—Large Hand-thrown Jars.

Page 23—Large Hand-thrown Jars.

Page 24—Large Hand-thrown Jars.

Page 25—Large Jar and Bowl in Wrought Iron Stands.

Page 26—Art and Gift Novelties.

Page 27—Tea Room Novelties.

Page 28—Art and Gift Novelties, Flower Pot and Hand-thrown Jar.

Page 29—Vases, Bowls, and Insets.

Page 30—Zasko Ware.

Page 31—Rubble Ware.

Page 32—Bird Baths.

Page 33—Gazing Globe, Sun Dial, and Bird Bath.

Page 34—Garden Jar, Porch Pot, Hanging Basket.

Page 35—Villa Pot, Garden Pot, and Italian Pot.

Page 36—Sand Jars.

Page 37—Hotel, Kitchen, and Utility Ware.

Catalog #9.

175

No. 22

Matt Green Italian Pot and Jardinieres and Pedestals

No. 23

The Italian Pot is an especially popular pot, being usually sold in pairs for the adornment of steps, approaches, and so forth.

No. 22 Jardiniere and Pedestal, Matt Green, 16-in. Pedestal with 9-in. Jardiniere. 20-in. Pedestal with 10-in. Jardiniere.
No. 22 Jardiniere only, Matt Green, 7, 8, 9, and 10 in.
No. 23 Jardiniere and Pedestal, Matt Green, 16-in. Pedestal with 9-in. Jardiniere. 20-in. Pedestal with 10-in. Jardiniere.
No. 23 Jardiniere only, Matt Green, 9 and 10 in.
No. 200 Italian Pot and Saucer, Matt Green, 9, 13, 16 and 21 in.

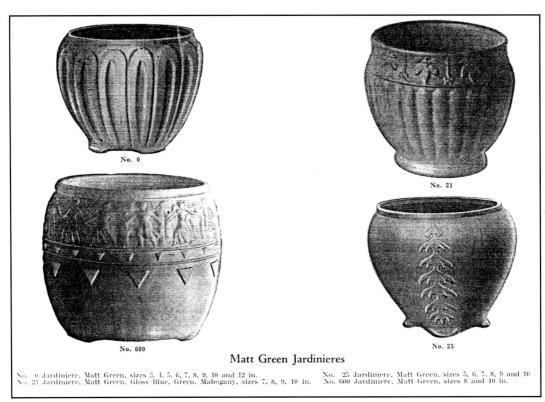

No. 0

No. 21

No. 600

No. 25

Matt Green Jardinieres

No. 0 Jardiniere, Matt Green, sizes 3, 4, 5, 6, 7, 8, 9, 10 and 12 in.
No. 21 Jardiniere, Matt Green, Gloss Blue, Green, Mahogany, sizes 7, 8, 9, 10 in.
No. 25 Jardiniere, Matt Green, sizes 5, 6, 7, 8, 9 and 10
No. 600 Jardiniere, Matt Green, sizes 8 and 10 in.

Catalog #9.

176

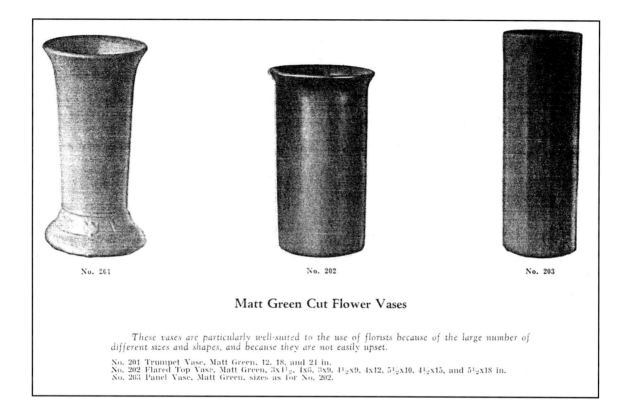

No. 201   No. 202   No. 203

Matt Green Cut Flower Vases

These vases are particularly well-suited to the use of florists because of the large number of different sizes and shapes, and because they are not easily upset.

No. 201 Trumpet Vase, Matt Green, 12, 18, and 21 in.
No. 202 Flared Top Vase, Matt Green, 3x1½, 4x6, 3x9, 4½x9, 4x12, 5½x10, 4½x15, and 5½x18 in.
No. 203 Panel Vase, Matt Green, sizes as for No. 202.

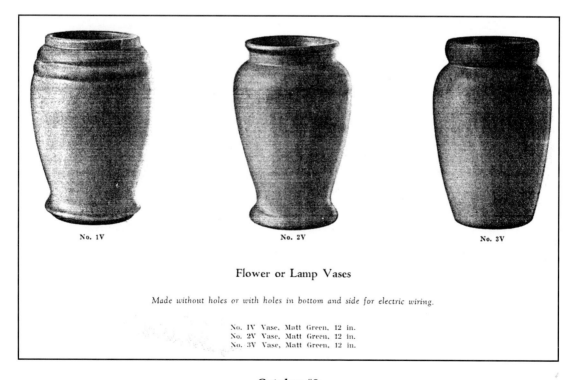

No. 1V   No. 2V   No. 3V

Flower or Lamp Vases

Made without holes or with holes in bottom and side for electric wiring.

No. 1V Vase, Matt Green, 12 in.
No. 2V Vase, Matt Green, 12 in.
No. 3V Vase, Matt Green, 12 in.

Catalog #9.

177

Cemetery and Wall Vases, Flower Pot, Fern Dishes, Specialties

No. 204 Cemetery Vase, Matt Green, 10 in. (Made with or without hole for hanging.)
No. 205 Wall Vase, Matt Green, 8 in.
No. 206 Flower Pot and Saucer, Matt Green, 2½, 3, 4, 5, 6, 7, 8, 9, and 10 in.
(No. 206 may be ordered also with the Saucer attached.)

No. 207 Low Flower Bowl, High Feet, Matt Green, 7, 8, and 9 in.
No. 208 Fern Dish, Matt Green, 7 and 9 in., with liner.
No. 209 Fern Dish, Matt Green, 5, 6, 7, and 8 in., with liner.
No. 214 Ash and Match Tray, Matt Green, 4¾ in.
No. 215 Cigar Jar, Matt Green, 6¾ in.

Umbrella or Sand Jars

No. 2 is shown also on page 36 in Stone finish, with green decoration around the top.

No. 1 Umbrella or Sand Jar, Matt Green, Bristol White, 10x21 in.
No. 2 Umbrella or Sand Jar, Matt Green, Bristol White, 10x21 in.

Catalog #9.

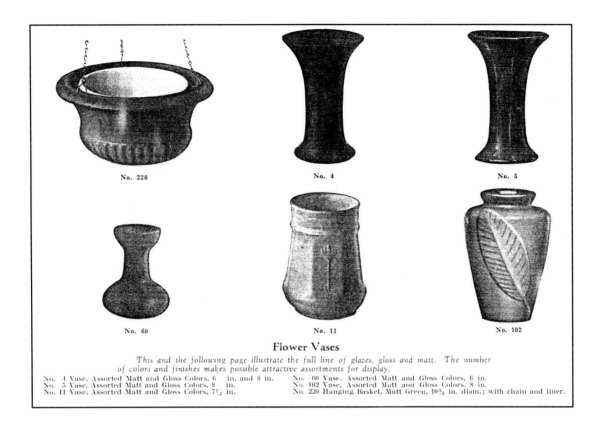

No. 220   No. 4   No. 5

No. 60   No. 11   No. 102

Flower Vases

This and the following page illustrate the full line of glazes, gloss and matt. The number
of colors and finishes makes possible attractive assortments for display.

No. 4 Vase, Assorted Matt and Gloss Colors, 6 in. and 8 in.   No. 60 Vase, Assorted Matt and Gloss Colors, 6 in.
No. 5 Vase, Assorted Matt and Gloss Colors, 8 in.   No. 102 Vase, Assorted Matt and Gloss Colors, 8 in.
No. 11 Vase, Assorted Matt and Gloss Colors, 7½ in.   No. 220 Hanging Basket, Matt Green, 10¾ in. diam.; with chain and liner.

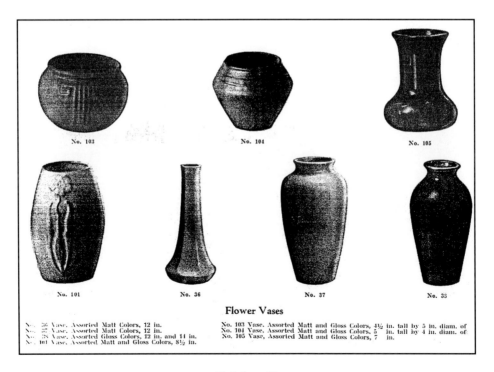

No. 103   No. 104   No. 105

No. 101   No. 36   No. 37   No. 38

Flower Vases

No. 36 Vase, Assorted Matt Colors, 12 in.   No. 103 Vase, Assorted Matt and Gloss Colors, 4½ in. tall by 5 in. diam. of
No. 37 Vase, Assorted Matt Colors, 12 in.   No. 104 Vase, Assorted Matt and Gloss Colors, 5 in. tall by 4 in. diam. of
No. 38 Vase, Assorted Gloss Colors, 12 in. and 14 in.   No. 105 Vase, Assorted Matt and Gloss Colors, 7 in.
No. 101 Vase, Assorted Matt and Gloss Colors, 8½ in.

Catalog #9.

179

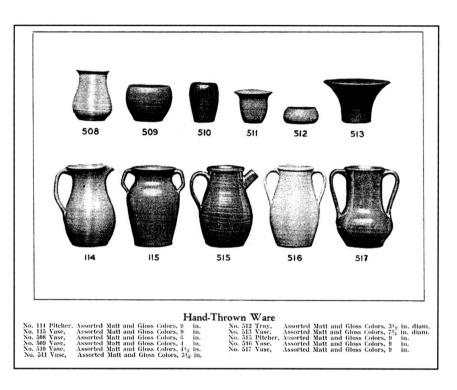

Hand-Thrown Ware

No. 111 Pitcher, Assorted Matt and Gloss Colors, 9 in.
No. 115 Vase, Assorted Matt and Gloss Colors, 9 in.
No. 508 Vase, Assorted Matt and Gloss Colors, 6 in.
No. 509 Vase, Assorted Matt and Gloss Colors, 4 in.
No. 510 Vase, Assorted Matt and Gloss Colors, 4½ in.
No. 511 Vase, Assorted Matt and Gloss Colors, 3½ in.

No. 512 Tray, Assorted Matt and Gloss Colors, 3½ in. diam.
No. 513 Vase, Assorted Matt and Gloss Colors, 7¾ in. diam.
No. 515 Pitcher, Assorted Matt and Gloss Colors, 9 in.
No. 516 Vase, Assorted Matt and Gloss Colors, 9 in.
No. 517 Vase, Assorted Matt and Gloss Colors, 9 in.

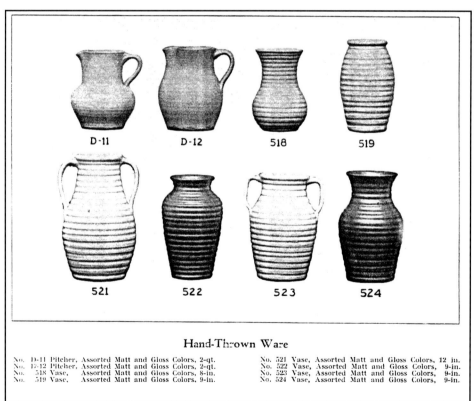

Hand-Thrown Ware

No. D-11 Pitcher, Assorted Matt and Gloss Colors, 2-qt.
No. D-12 Pitcher, Assorted Matt and Gloss Colors, 2-qt.
No. 518 Vase, Assorted Matt and Gloss Colors, 8-in.
No. 519 Vase, Assorted Matt and Gloss Colors, 9-in.

No. 521 Vase, Assorted Matt and Gloss Colors, 12 in.
No. 522 Vase, Assorted Matt and Gloss Colors, 9-in.
No. 523 Vase, Assorted Matt and Gloss Colors, 9-in.
No. 524 Vase, Assorted Matt and Gloss Colors, 9-in.

Catalog #9.

Art and Gift Novelties, Hand-Thrown Vases

The No. 722 Gazing Globe is designed as an ornament for the interior, the library or den. The base, the modeling on which depicts the Hindu Crystal Gazer, carries with it a suggestion of the mysterious art of the East.

No. 577 Hand-thrown Vase, Gloss Green, 7, 10, and 11 in.
No. 578 Pitcher, Assorted Matt and Gloss Colors, 2½ in.
No. 579 Pitcher, Assorted Matt and Gloss Colors, 4-pint.
No. 580 Tumbler, Assorted Matt and Gloss Colors, 8-oz. 4¾ in. tall.

No. 581 Hand-thrown Pitcher, Assorted Matt and Gloss Colors. 3-pint, 6 in. tall.
No. 712 Jardiniere, Gloss Lavender, 5, 6, 7, 8, 9, and 10 in.
No. 720 Hand-thrown Vase, Assorted Matt and Gloss Colors, 9-in.
No. 722 Gazing Globe and Base, 12 in. high. Globe 7 in. Base 5½ in. Base is in Mottled Grayish Buff finish.

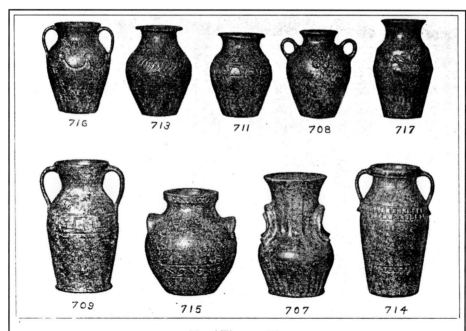

Hand-Thrown Ware

The charm of these lovely hand-thrown shapes is enhanced by the hand-marking and hand-finishing. The finish is a neutral grayish-buff mottled effect, like that of the large Oil Jars on Pages 16 and 17.

No. 707 Vase, 11½ in.
No. 708 Vase, 9 in.
No. 709 Vase, 12½ in.

No. 711 Vase, 8½ in.
No. 713 Vase, 9 in.
No. 714 Vase, 12½ in.

No. 715 Vase, 10 in.
No. 716 Vase, 9 in.
No. 717 Vase, 10 in.

Catalog #9.

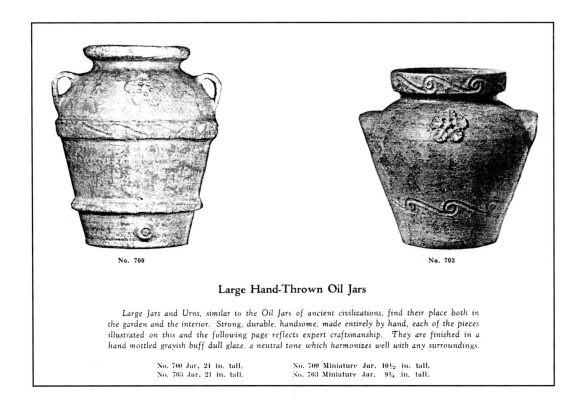

No. 700   No. 703

Large Hand-Thrown Oil Jars

Large Jars and Urns, similar to the Oil Jars of ancient civilizations, find their place both in the garden and the interior. Strong, durable, handsome, made entirely by hand, each of the pieces illustrated on this and the following page reflects expert craftsmanship. They are finished in a hand mottled grayish buff dull glaze, a neutral tone which harmonizes well with any surroundings.

No. 700 Jar, 24 in. tall.   No. 700 Miniature Jar, 10½ in. tall.
No. 703 Jar, 21 in. tall.   No. 703 Miniature Jar, 9¾ in. tall.

No. 701   No. 702

Large Hand-Thrown Oil Jars

Miniature sizes of the large Oil Jars on this page and Page 16, reproduced by hand in exact detail, make beautiful Lamp or Flower Vases, and form an addition to the simpler designs illustrated on Page 15.

No. 701 Jar, 26 in. tall.   No. 701 Miniature Jar, 12 in. tall.
No. 702 Jar, 33 in. tall.   No. 702 Miniature Jar, 13½ in. tall.

Catalog #9.

Large Hand-Thrown Jars

No. 109 Assorted Matt and Gloss Colors, 21 in. tall; Diameter of opening, 5¾ in.
No. 111 Assorted Matt and Gloss Colors, 21 in. tall; Diameter of opening, 5¾ in.
No. 112 Assorted Matt and Gloss Colors, 21 in. tall; Diameter of opening, 7¼ in.

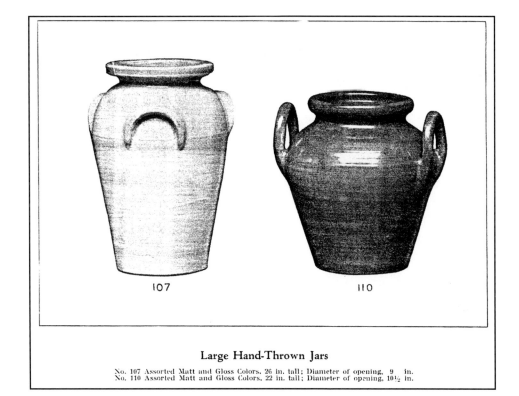

Large Hand-Thrown Jars

No. 107 Assorted Matt and Gloss Colors, 26 in. tall; Diameter of opening, 9 in.
No. 110 Assorted Matt and Gloss Colors, 22 in. tall; Diameter of opening, 10½ in.

Catalog #9.

183

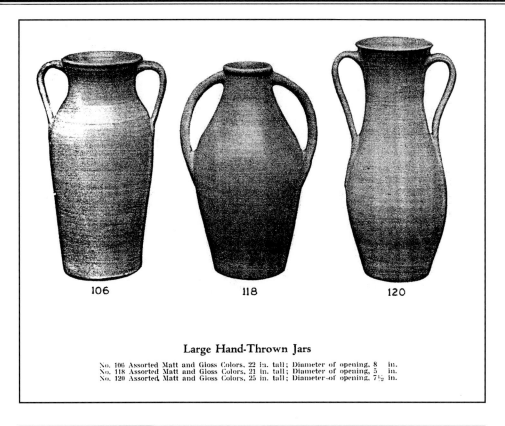

Large Hand-Thrown Jars

No. 106 Assorted Matt and Gloss Colors, 22 in. tall; Diameter of opening, 8 in.
No. 118 Assorted Matt and Gloss Colors, 21 in. tall; Diameter of opening, 5 in.
No. 120 Assorted Matt and Gloss Colors, 25 in. tall; Diameter of opening, 7½ in.

Large Hand-Thrown Jars

No. 562 Assorted Matt and Gloss Colors, 32 in. tall; Diameter of opening, 6½ in.
No. 704 Assorted Matt and Gloss Colors, 23 in. tall; Diameter of opening, 10 in.

Catalog #9.

184

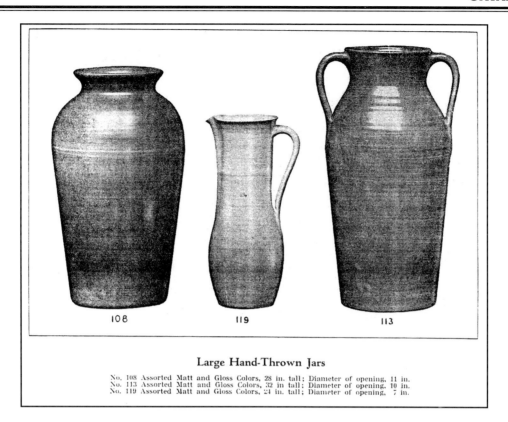

Large Hand-Thrown Jars

No. 108 Assorted Matt and Gloss Colors, 28 in. tall; Diameter of opening, 11 in.
No. 113 Assorted Matt and Gloss Colors, 32 in. tall; Diameter of opening, 10 in.
No. 119 Assorted Matt and Gloss Colors, 24 in. tall; Diameter of opening, 7 in.

Large Hand-Thrown Jars

No. 710 Assorted Matt and Gloss Colors, 14 in. tall by 21 in. extreme diameter;
Diameter of opening, 11½ in.
No. 721 Assorted Matt and Gloss Colors, 23 in. tall; Diameter of opening, 11 in.

Catalog #9.

Large Hand-Thrown Jars

No. 719 Jar illustrates the run over glazes, this one a dark blue over a light gray. For Jars ordered in run over glazes, 10 percent extra is charged.

No. 718 Assorted Matt and Gloss Colors, 26 in. tall; Diameter of opening, 10 in.
No. 719 Assorted Matt and Gloss Colors, 27 in. tall; Diameter of opening, 10½ in.

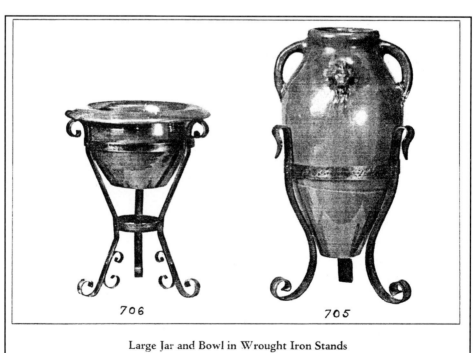

Large Jar and Bowl in Wrought Iron Stands

No. 705 Jar, with Hammered Iron Stand, Assorted Matt and Gloss Colors, 30 in. extreme height. Height of Jar, 26 in. Diameter of opening, 6½ in. Jar is made with or without handles.

No. 706 Bowl, with Iron Stand, Assorted Matt and Gloss Colors, 20½ in. extreme height. Outside diameter of Bowl, 16½ in. Inside diameter, 11½ in.

Catalog #9.

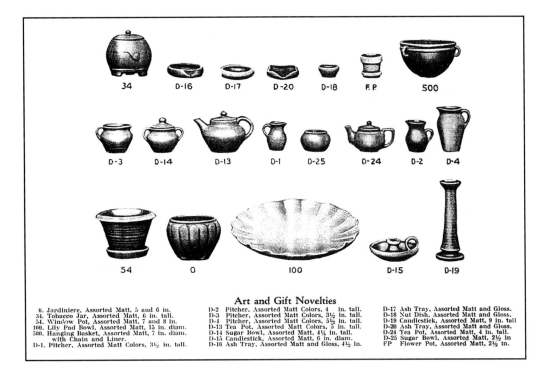

Art and Gift Novelties

0. Jardiniere, Assorted Matt, 5 and 6 in.
34. Tobacco Jar, Assorted Matt, 6 in. tall.
54. Window Pot, Assorted Matt, 7 and 8 in.
100. Lily Pad Bowl, Assorted Matt, 15 in. diam.
500. Hanging Basket, Assorted Matt, 7 in. diam. with Chain and Liner.
D-1. Pitcher, Assorted Matt Colors, 3½ in. tall.

D-2 Pitcher, Assorted Matt Colors, 4 in. tall.
D-3 Pitcher, Assorted Matt Colors, 3½ in. tall.
D-4 Pitcher, Assorted Matt Colors, 5½ in. tall.
D-13 Tea Pot, Assorted Matt Colors, 5 in. tall.
D-14 Sugar Bowl, Assorted Matt, 4¼ in. tall.
D-15 Candlestick, Assorted Matt, 6 in. diam.
D-16 Ash Tray, Assorted Matt and Gloss, 4½ in.

D-17 Ash Tray, Assorted Matt and Gloss.
D-18 Nut Dish, Assorted Matt and Gloss.
D-19 Candlestick, Assorted Matt, 9 in. tall
D-20 Ash Tray, Assorted Matt and Gloss.
D-24 Tea Pot, Assorted Matt, 4 in. tall.
D-25 Sugar Bowl, Assorted Matt, 2½ in
FP Flower Pot, Assorted Matt, 2½ in.

Art and Gift Novelties, Flower Pot, Hand-Thrown Jar

No. 96. Bowl, Stone finish with Green decoration, 8 in.
No. 555 Bowl, Assorted Matt Colors, 11 in., high and low shape.
No. 556 Candlestick, Assorted Matt Colors, 4 in. diam.

No. 557 Match Holder, Assorted Matt Colors, 2 in tall.
No. 558 Hand-thrown Jar, Assorted Matt and Gloss Colors, 15
No. 560 Flower Pot, Matt Green, 5, 6, 7, 8, 9 and 10 in.

Catalog #9.

187

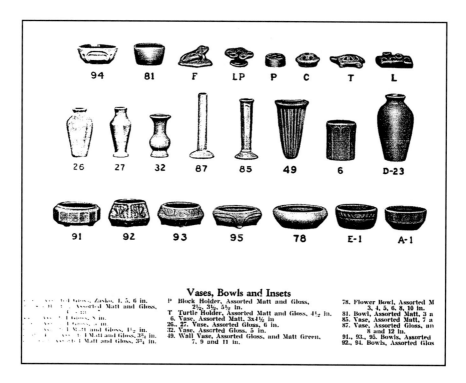

Vases, Bowls and Insets

. . . . Gloss, Zasko, 4. 5, 6 in.	P Block Holder, Assorted Matt and Gloss, 2½, 3½, 5½ in.	78. Flower Bowl, Assorted M 3, 4, 5, 6, 8, 10 in.
. . . . . . Assorted Matt and Gloss, ... 33	T Turtle Holder, Assorted Matt and Gloss, 4½ in.	81. Bowl, Assorted Matt, 3 a
. . . . . d Gloss, 8 in.	6. Vase, Assorted Matt, 3x4½ in	85. Vase, Assorted Matt, 7 a
. . . . . d Gloss, 2 in.	26., 27. Vase, Assorted Gloss, 6 in.	87. Vase, Assorted Gloss, an
. . . . . d Matt and Gloss, 1½ in.	32. Vase, Assorted Gloss. 5 in.	8 and 12 in.
. . . . . Assorted Matt and Gloss, 3¾ in.	49. Wall Vase, Assorted Gloss, and Matt Green, 7, 9 and 11 in.	91., 93., 95. Bowls, Assorted
. . . . . ssorted Matt and Gloss, 3¾ in.		92., 94. Bowls, Assorted Glos

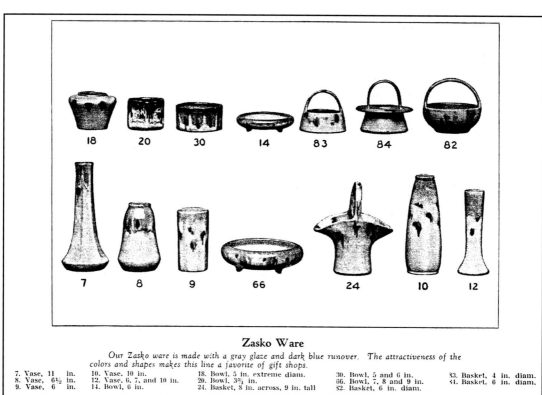

Zasko Ware

Our Zasko ware is made with a gray glaze and dark blue runover. The attractiveness of the colors and shapes makes this line a favorite of gift shops.

7. Vase, 11 in.	10. Vase. 10 in.	18. Bowl, 5 in. extreme diam.	30. Bowl, 5 and 6 in.	83. Basket, 4 in. diam.
8. Vase, 6½ in.	12. Vase, 6, 7, and 10 in.	20. Bowl, 3¾ in.	66. Bowl, 7, 8 and 9 in.	84. Basket, 6 in. diam.
9. Vase, 6 in.	14. Bowl, 6 in.	24. Basket, 8 in. across, 9 in. tall	82. Basket, 6 in. diam.	

Catalog #9.

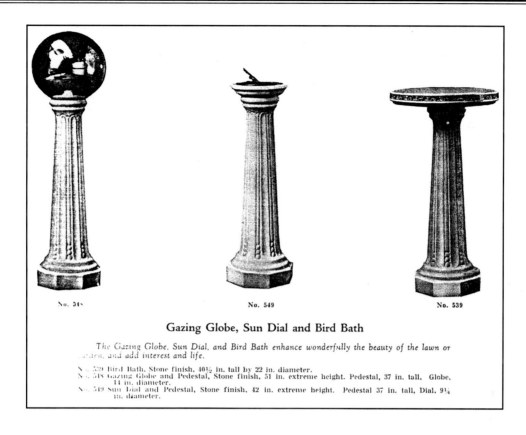

No. 548   No. 549   No. 539

Gazing Globe, Sun Dial and Bird Bath

The Gazing Globe, Sun Dial, and Bird Bath enhance wonderfully the beauty of the lawn or garden, and add interest and life.

No. 539 Bird Bath, Stone finish, 40½ in. tall by 22 in. diameter.
No. 548 Gazing Globe and Pedestal, Stone finish, 51 in. extreme height. Pedestal, 37 in. tall. Globe, 14 in. diameter.
No. 549 Sun Dial and Pedestal, Stone finish, 42 in. extreme height. Pedestal 37 in. tall, Dial, 9¾ in. diameter.

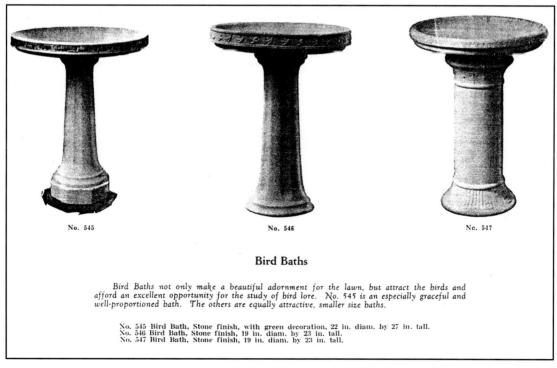

No. 545   No. 546   No. 547

Bird Baths

Bird Baths not only make a beautiful adornment for the lawn, but attract the birds and afford an excellent opportunity for the study of bird lore. No. 545 is an especially graceful and well-proportioned bath. The others are equally attractive, smaller size baths.

No. 545 Bird Bath, Stone finish, with green decoration, 22 in. diam. by 27 in. tall.
No. 546 Bird Bath, Stone finish, 19 in. diam. by 23 in. tall.
No. 547 Bird Bath, Stone finish, 19 in. diam. by 23 in. tall.

Catalog #9.

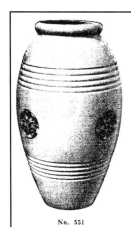  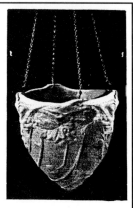

No. 551   No. 542   No. 543

Garden Jar, Porch Pot, Hanging Basket

No. 551 is a useful and decorative jar for lawns and formal gardens. No. 542 Porch Pot may be used as a jardiniere or makes a convenient catch-all for the porch. Hanging Basket No. 543 is designed for direct planting.

No. 542 Porch Pot. Stone finish, 18½ in. diam.
No. 543 Hanging Basket. Stone finish, 10 in. diam. (chain included.)
No. 551 Garden Jar, Stone finish or Green Gloss, 24 and 30 in.

No. 540   No. 550   No. 541

Villa Pot, Garden Pot and Italian Pot

These are handsome pots for porch approaches, pedestals of balustrades. and so forth. No. 540 and 550 also make excellent Sand Jars for hotels, clubs, and similar institutions. Please see the illustration of No. 550 in Matt Rose on Page 36.

No. 540 Villa Pot, Stone finish, with green decoration, 16 and 22 in. Saucer extra if desired.
No. 541 Italian Pot and Saucer, Stone finish, 9, 13, 16 and 21 in.
No. 550 Garden Pot, Stone finish, with green decoration, 16 in.

Catalog #9.

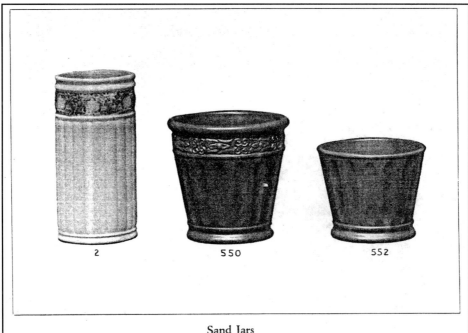

Sand Jars

The items illustrated here, together with Nos. 540 and 550 on Page 35, offer a wide selection of Sand Jars. No. 550, glazed in a beautiful Matt Rose, may be used as a Jardiniere.

No. 2 Sand Jar, Stone finish, with green decoration, 10x21 in.
No. 550 Jar, Matt Rose and Stone finish, with green decoration, 16 in.
No. 552 Jar, Matt Rose, 14 in.

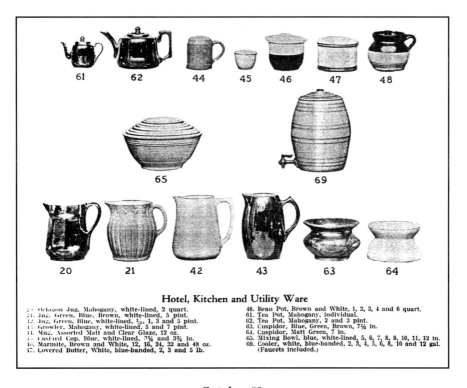

Hotel, Kitchen and Utility Ware

20. Octagon Jug, Mahogany, white-lined, 2 quart.
21. Jug, Green, Blue, Brown, white-lined, 5 pint.
42. Jug, Green, Blue, white-lined, ½, 1, 3 and 5 pint.
43. Growler, Mahogany, white-lined, 5 and 7 pint.
44. Mug, Assorted Matt and Clear Glaze, 12 oz.
45. Custard Cup, Blue, white-lined, 3¼ and 3¾ in.
46. Marmite, Brown and White, 12, 16, 24, 32 and 48 oz.
47. Covered Butter, White, blue-banded, 2, 3 and 5 lb.

48. Bean Pot, Brown and White, 1, 2, 3, and 6 quart.
61. Tea Pot, Mahogany, individual.
62. Tea Pot, Mahogany, 2 and 3 pint.
63. Cuspidor, Blue, Green, Brown, 7½ in.
64. Cuspidor, Matt Green, 7 in.
65. Mixing Bowl, blue, white-lined, 5, 6, 7, 8, 9, 10, 11, 12 in.
69. Cooler, white, blue-banded, 2, 3, 4, 5, 6, 8, 10 and 12 gal.
(Faucets included.)

Catalog #9.

191

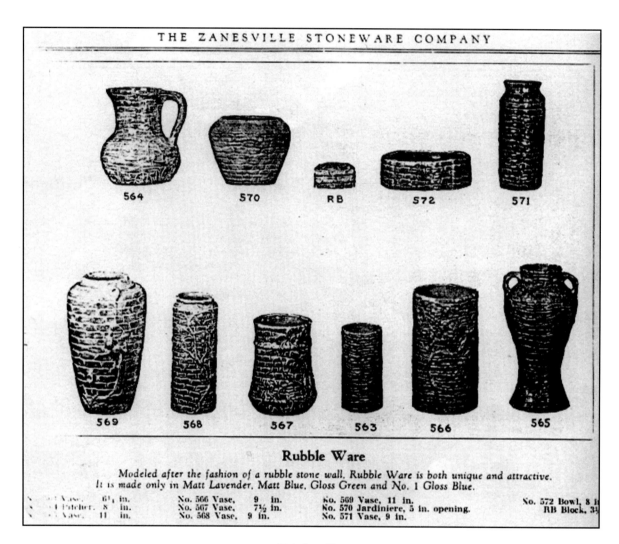

THE ZANESVILLE STONEWARE COMPANY

564   570   RB   572   571

569   568   567   563   566   565

Rubble Ware

Modeled after the fashion of a rubble stone wall, Rubble Ware is both unique and attractive. It is made only in Matt Lavender, Matt Blue, Gloss Green and No. 1 Gloss Blue.

No. ... Vase, 6½ in.	No. 566 Vase, 9 in.	No. 569 Vase, 11 in.	No. 572 Bowl, 8 i...
No. ... Pitcher, 8 in.	No. 567 Vase, 7½ in.	No. 570 Jardiniere, 5 in. opening.	RB Block, 3¼
No. ... Vase, 11 in.	No. 568 Vase, 9 in.	No. 571 Vase, 9 in.	

Catalog #9.

192

PRICE LIST

Prices are for goods crated free, F. O. B. Zanesville.

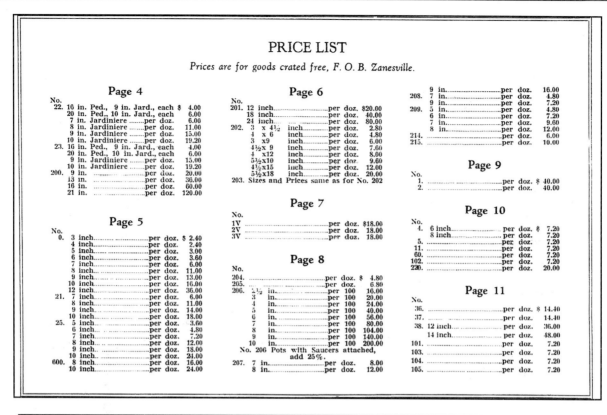

Page 4
No.
22.	16 in. Ped., 9 in. Jard., each	$ 4.00
	20 in. Ped., 10 in. Jard., each	6.00
	7 in. Jardiniere ......per doz.	6.00
	8 in. Jardiniere ......per doz.	11.00
	9 in. Jardiniere ......per doz.	15.00
	10 in. Jardiniere ......per doz.	19.20
23.	16 in. Ped., 9 in. Jard., each	4.00
	20 in. Ped., 10 in. Jard., each	6.00
	9 in. Jardiniere ......per doz.	15.00
	10 in. Jardiniere ......per doz.	19.20
200.	9 in. ......per doz.	20.00
	13 in. ......per doz.	36.00
	16 in. ......per doz.	60.00
	21 in. ......per doz.	120.00

Page 5
No.
0.	3 inch......per doz.	$ 2.40
	4 inch......per doz.	2.40
	5 inch......per doz.	3.00
	6 inch......per doz.	3.60
	7 inch......per doz.	6.00
	8 inch......per doz.	11.00
	9 inch......per doz.	13.00
	10 inch......per doz.	16.00
	12 inch......per doz.	36.00
21.	7 inch......per doz.	6.00
	8 inch......per doz.	11.00
	9 inch......per doz.	14.00
	10 inch......per doz.	18.00
25.	5 inch......per doz.	3.60
	6 inch......per doz.	4.80
	7 inch......per doz.	7.20
	8 inch......per doz.	12.00
	9 inch......per doz.	18.00
	10 inch......per doz.	24.00
600.	8 inch......per doz.	16.00
	10 inch......per doz.	24.00

Page 6
No.
201.	12 inch......per doz.	$20.00
	18 inch......per doz.	40.00
	24 inch......per doz.	80.00
202.	3 x 4½ inch......per doz.	2.80
	4 x 6 inch......per doz.	4.80
	3 x9 inch......per doz.	6.00
	4½x 9 inch......per doz.	7.60
	4 x12 inch......per doz.	8.00
	5½x10 inch......per doz.	9.60
	4½x15 inch......per doz.	12.00
	5½x18 inch......per doz.	20.00
203.	Sizes and Prices same as for No. 202	

Page 7
No.
1V	......per doz.	$18.00
2V	......per doz.	18.00
3V	......per doz.	18.00

Page 8
No.
204.	......per doz.	$ 4.80
205.	......per doz.	6.80
206.	2½ in. ......per 100	16.00
	3 in. ......per 100	20.00
	4 in. ......per 100	24.00
	5 in. ......per 100	40.00
	6 in. ......per 100	56.00
	7 in. ......per 100	80.00
	8 in. ......per 100	104.00
	9 in. ......per 100	140.00
	10 in. ......per 100	200.00

No. 206 Pots with Saucers attached, add 25%.
| 207. | 7 in. ......per doz. | 8.00 |
| | 8 in. ......per doz. | 12.00 |

208.	9 in. ......per doz.	16.00
	7 in. ......per doz.	4.80
	9 in. ......per doz.	7.20
209.	5 in. ......per doz.	4.80
	6 in. ......per doz.	7.20
	7 in. ......per doz.	9.60
	8 in. ......per doz.	12.00
214.	......per doz.	6.00
215.	......per doz.	10.00

Page 9
No.
| 1. | ......per doz. | $ 40.00 |
| 2. | ......per doz. | 40.00 |

Page 10
No.
4.	6 inch......per doz.	$ 7.20
	8 inch......per doz.	7.20
5.	......per doz.	7.20
11.	......per doz.	7.20
60.	......per doz.	7.20
102.	......per doz.	7.20
220.	......per doz.	20.00

Page 11
No.
36.	......per doz.	$ 14.40
37.	......per doz.	14.40
38.	12 inch......per doz.	36.00
	14 inch......per doz.	48.00
101.	......per doz.	7.20
103.	......per doz.	7.20
104.	......per doz.	7.20
105.	......per doz.	7.20

Page 12
No.
114.	......per doz.	$ 24.00
115.	......per doz.	24.00
508.	......per doz.	12.00
509.	......per doz.	6.00
510.	......per doz.	4.00
511.	......per doz.	3.60
512.	......per doz.	3.00
513.	......per doz.	12.00
515.	......per doz.	30.00
516.	......per doz.	24.00
517.	......per doz.	24.00

Page 13
No.
D-11.	......per doz.	$ 18.00
D-12.	......per doz.	18.00
518.	......per doz.	18.00
519.	......per doz.	18.00
521.	......per doz.	36.00
522.	......per doz.	20.00
523.	......per doz.	24.00
524.	......per doz.	20.00

Page 14
No.
577.	7 in. ......per doz.	$ 8.00
	10 in. ......per doz.	14.40
	11 in. ......per doz.	20.00
578.	......per doz.	3.00
579.	......per doz.	12.00
580.	......per doz.	3.00
581.	......per doz.	12.00
712.	5 in. ......per doz.	4.80
	6 in. ......per doz.	7.20
	7 in. ......per doz.	9.60
	8 in. ......per doz.	12.00
	9 in. ......per doz.	15.36
	10 in. ......per doz.	19.20
720.	......per doz.	30.00
722.	......each	6.00

Page 15
No.
707.	......per doz.	$ 96.00
708.	......per doz.	60.00
709.	......per doz.	84.00
711.	......per doz.	48.00
713.	......per doz.	48.00
714.	......per doz.	72.00
715.	......per doz.	96.00
716.	......per doz.	60.00
717.	......per doz.	60.00

Page 16
No.
700.	Oil Jar......each	$ 40.00
703.	Oil Jar......each	30.00
700.	Miniature ......each	10.00
703.	Miniature ......each	8.00

Page 17
No.
701.	Oil Jar......each	$ 50.00
702.	Oil Jar......each	50.00
701.	Miniature ......each	12.00
702.	Miniature ......each	12.00

Page 18
No.
109.	......each	$ 12.00
111.	......each	12.00
112.	......each	10.00

Page 19
No.
106.	......each	$ 15.00
118.	......each	12.00
120.	......each	20.00

Page 20
No.
| 107. | ......each | $ 30.00 |
| 110. | ......each | 30.00 |

Page 21
No.
108.	......each	$ 20.00
113.	......each	25.00
119.	......each	15.00

Page 22
No.
| 562. | ......each | 25.00 |
| 704. | ......each | 25.00 |

Page 23
No.
| 718. | ......each | $ 25.00 |
| 719. | ......each | 20.00 |

For Jars in run-over glazes, add 10%.

Page 24
No.
| 710. | ......each | $ 20.00 |
| 711. | ......each | 25.00 |

Page 25
No.
| 705. | ......each | $ 27.00 |
| 706. | ......each | 10.00 |

Catalog #9.

THE ZANESVILLE STONEWARE COMPANY

Page 26

No.			
0.	5 inch	per doz.	$ 3.60
	6 inch	per doz.	4.32
34.		per doz.	10.00
54.	7 inch, without saucer	per doz.	9.00
	7 inch, with saucer	per doz.	12.00
	8 inch, without saucer	per doz.	12.00
	8 inch, with saucer	per doz.	15.00
100.		per doz.	48.00
500.		per doz.	18.00
D-1		per doz.	3.00
D-2		per doz.	3.00
D-3		per doz.	5.00
D-4		per doz.	5.00
D-13		per doz.	8.00
D-14	with cover	per doz.	6.00
	without cover	per doz.	5.00
D-15		per doz.	7.20
D-16		per doz.	3.00
D-17		per doz.	3.00
D-18		per doz.	.89
D-19		per doz.	12.00
D-20		per doz.	3.00
D-24		per doz.	6.00
D-25		per doz.	3.60
FP		per doz.	1.92

Page 27

No.			
50.		per doz.	$ 3.00
51.		per doz.	4.80
52.		per doz.	7.20
561.		per doz.	12.00
574.		per doz.	7.20
575.		per doz.	9.00

Page 28

No.			
96.		per doz.	$ 12.00
555.	low shape	per doz.	20.00
	high shape	per doz.	24.00
556.		per doz.	6.00
557.		per doz.	3.60
558.		per doz.	72.00
560.	5 inch	per doz.	6.00
	6 inch	per doz.	9.00
	7 inch	per doz.	12.00
	8 inch	per doz.	15.00
	9 inch	per doz.	19.20
	10 inch	per doz.	24.00
560.	Pots without Saucers, deduct 20%.		

Page 29

A-1	4 inch	per doz.	$ 2.80
	5 inch	per doz.	4.00
	6 inch	per doz.	4.80
C	2½ inch	per doz.	3.60
	3½ inch	per doz.	6.00
	4 inch	per doz.	9.00
	5 inch	per doz.	12.00
D-23		per doz.	9.00
E-1		per doz.	3.60
F		per doz.	8.00
L		per doz.	6.00
LP		per doz.	8.00
P	2½ inch	per doz.	3.60
	3½ inch	per doz.	4.80
	5½ inch	per doz.	7.20
T		per doz.	6.00
6.	3x4½ inch	per doz.	3.36
26.		per doz.	6.00
27.		per doz.	6.00
32.		per doz.	6.00
49.	7 inch	per doz.	6.00
	9 inch	per doz.	9.00
	11 inch	per doz.	12.00

78.	3	inch	per doz.	3.00
	4	inch	per doz.	3.50
	5	inch	per doz.	4.00
	6	inch	per doz.	6.00
	8	inch	per doz.	10.00
	10	inch	per doz.	16.00
81.	3	inch	per doz.	3.00
85.	5	inch	per doz.	5.00
	7	inch	per doz.	6.00
	10	inch	per doz.	12.00
87.	8	inch	per doz.	6.00
	12	inch	per doz.	12.00
91.			per doz.	6.00
92.			per doz.	6.00
93.			per doz.	6.00
94.			per doz.	3.60
95.			per doz.	6.00

Page 30

No.			
7.		per doz.	$ 24.00
8.		per doz.	12.00
9.		per doz.	6.00
10.		per doz.	24.00
12.	6 inch	per doz.	6.00
	7 inch	per doz.	12.00
	10 inch	per doz.	18.00
14.		per doz.	6.00
18.		per doz.	6.00
20.		per doz.	6.00
24.		per doz.	18.00
30.	5 inch	per doz.	6.00
	6 inch	per doz.	9.00
66.	7 inch	per doz.	12.00
	8 inch	per doz.	16.00
	9 inch	per doz.	24.00
82.		per doz.	12.00
83		per doz.	6.00
84.		per doz.	12.00

THE ZANESVILLE STONEWARE COMPANY

Page 31

No.		
563.	per doz.	$ 8.00
564.	per doz.	24.00
565.	per doz.	26.40
566.	per doz.	18.00
567.	per doz.	14.40
568.	per doz.	14.40
569.	per doz.	30.00
570.	per doz.	10.00
571.	per doz.	12.00
572.	per doz.	12.00
RB	per doz.	6.00

Page 32

No.		
545.	each	$ 15.00
546.	each	12.00
547.	each	12.00

Page 33

No.		
539.	each	$ 22.50
548.	each	30.00
549.	each	25.00

Page 34

No.			
542.		each	$ 12.00
543.		per doz.	24.00
551.	24 inch	each	12.00
	30 inch	each	24.00

Page 35

No.			
540.	16 inch	each	$ 5.00
	22 inch	each	15.00
541.	9 inch	per doz.	20.00
	13 inch	per doz.	36.00
	16 inch	per doz.	60.00
	21 inch	per doz.	120.00
550.		each	5.00

Page 36

No.		
2.	per doz.	$ 48.00
550.	per doz.	60.00
552.	per doz.	48.00

Page 37

No.			
20.		per doz.	$ 4.40
21.		per doz.	5.00
42.	½-pint	per doz.	3.60
	1 -pint	per doz.	4.80
	3 -pint	per doz.	6.00
	5 -pint	per doz.	8.00
43.	5 -pint	per doz.	4.40
	7 -pint	per doz.	4.80
44.		per doz.	2.50
45.	3¼-in.	per doz.	1.00
	3¾-in.	per doz.	1.20
46.	12 -oz	per doz.	1.50
	16 -oz	per doz.	2.00
	24 -oz.	per doz.	2.50

	32 -oz.	per doz.	3.34
	48 -oz.	per doz.	4.00
47.	2 -lb.	per doz.	3.60
	3 -lb.	per doz.	4.40
	5 -lb.	per doz.	6.00
48.	1 -qt.	per doz.	3.96
	2 -qt.	per doz.	4.86
	3 -qt.	per doz.	6.00
	4 -qt.	per doz.	7.20
	6 -qt.	per doz.	9.00
61.		per doz.	3.50
62.	2 -pt.	per doz.	5.00
	3 -pt.	per doz.	6.00
63.	7½-in.	per doz.	4.00
64.	7 -in.	per doz.	6.00
65.	5 -in.	per doz.	1.56
	6 -in.	per doz.	1.80
	7 -in.	per doz.	2.16
	8 -in.	per doz.	2.88
	9 -in.	per doz.	3.60
	10 -in.	per doz.	6.00
	11 -in.	per doz.	8.40
	12 -in.	per doz.	10.80
69.	2 -gal.	each	3.20
	3 -gal.	each	3.60
	4 -gal.	each	4.00
	5 -gal.	each	4.50
	6 -gal.	each	5.20
	8 -gal.	each	6.00
	10 -gal.	each	7.00
	12 -gal.	each	8.50

Catalog #9.

Foreword

.ALL the Ware illustrated in this catalogue is made in a hard-fired body, colored in a variety of glazes, gloss and matt. Strength and durability are therefore added to pleasing appearance.

COLORS

Colors are Matt Green, Matt Rose, Matt Lavender, Gloss Blue, Gloss Green, Gloss Rose, Gloss Black, Royal Blue, Mahogany, Mottled Buff, Zasko, and Bristol White. Some items are offered in certain colors only, which are specified in the descriptive matter. Where colors are listed as "Assorted Matt and Gloss," any color may be ordered. It must be borne in mind, however, that although we carry a large stock it is impossible to keep a full assortment at all times of so many colors; and if a large assortment of colors is specified, it may occasion a delay of two or three weeks in shipping. The full line of colors is shown on the opposite page.

Matt Green is illustrated by Nos. 101 and 102
Matt Rose is illustrated by Nos. 104 and 37
Matt Lavender is illustrated by No. 11
Royal Blue is illustrated by Nos. 4 and 576.
Gloss Blue is illustrated by No. 38
Gloss Green is illustrated by Nos. 105 and 795
Gloss Rose is illustrated by No. 5

Catalog #10.

MATT GREEN WARE

Attention is called to our Matt Green Ware, both the Jardinieres, Cut Flower Vases, and so forth, which are produced exclusively in that color, and the various items listed throughout the catalogue which may be ordered in Matt Green. Matt Green is the staple standby which never grows old and is continuous in its appeal to the most refined class of trade.

HAND-THROWN WARE

Attention is also directed to our line of genuine hand-made ware, turned up on a potter's wheel. The slight deviations and irregularities left by the potter's hands give to each piece individuality and beauty.

POTTERY FOR PORCH, LAWN AND GARDEN

Pages 14 to 23 show our pottery for interior and exterior decoration, both in colored glazes and in stone finish. The latter is a rough stone effect which is most attractive and accomodates itself to any surroundings.

HOTEL, KITCHEN AND UTILITY WARE

Items of Hotel, Kitchen and Utility Ware are illustrated on Page 24. In quality of workmanship and design, we believe these items to be unexcelled by any similar line.

Prices are for goods crated without extra charge, F. O. B. Zanesville, Ohio

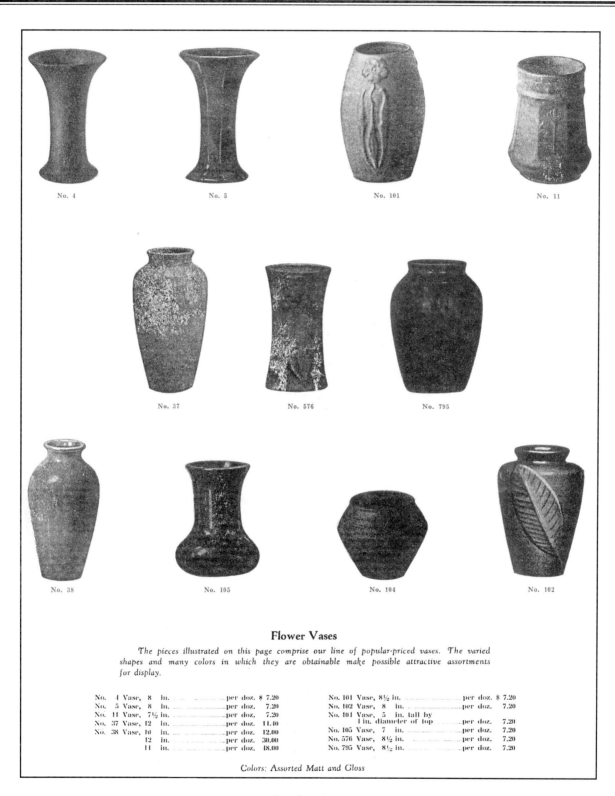

No. 4   No. 5   No. 101   No. 11

No. 37   No. 576   No. 795

No. 38   No. 105   No. 104   No. 102

Flower Vases

The pieces illustrated on this page comprise our line of popular-priced vases. The varied shapes and many colors in which they are obtainable make possible attractive assortments for display.

No. 4 Vase, 8 in. ....per doz. $ 7.20	No. 101 Vase, 8½ in. ....per doz. $ 7.20	
No. 5 Vase, 8 in. ....per doz. 7.20	No. 102 Vase, 8 in. ....per doz. 7.20	
No. 11 Vase, 7½ in. ....per doz. 7.20	No. 104 Vase, 5 in. tall by	
No. 37 Vase, 12 in. ....per doz. 14.40	4 in. diameter of top ......per doz. 7.20	
No. 38 Vase, 10 in. ....per doz. 12.00	No. 105 Vase, 7 in. ....per doz. 7.20	
12 in. ....per doz. 30.00	No. 576 Vase, 8½ in. ....per doz. 7.20	
14 in. ....per doz. 48.00	No. 795 Vase, 8½ in. ....per doz. 7.20	

Colors: Assorted Matt and Gloss

Catalog #10.

196

No. 22

No. 200

No. 23

No. 0

No. 25

No. 21

Matt Green Italian Pot and Jardinieres and Pedestals

The Italian Pot is an especially popular pot, being usually sold in pairs for the adornment of steps, approaches, and so forth.

No. 0 Jardiniere, Matt Green,

3 in.	per doz.	$ 2.40
4 in.	per doz.	2.40
5 in.	per doz.	3.00
6 in.	per doz.	3.60
7 in.	per doz.	6.00
8 in.	per doz.	11.00
9 in.	per doz.	13.00
10 in.	per doz.	16.00
12 in.	per doz.	36.00

No. 22 Jardiniere and Pedestal, Matt Green,

16 in. Ped., 9 in. Jard.,	each	$ 1.00
20 in. Ped., 10 in. Jard.,	each	6.00
7 in. Jardiniere	per doz.	6.00
8 in. Jardiniere	per doz.	11.00
9 in. Jardiniere	per doz.	15.00
10 in. Jardiniere	per doz.	19.20

No. 23 Jardiniere and Pedestal, Matt Green,

No. 25 Jardiniere, Matt Green,

5 in.	per doz.	$ 3.68
6 in.	per doz.	4.80
7 in.	per doz.	7.20
8 in.	per doz.	12.00
9 in.	per doz.	18.60
10 in.	per doz.	24.00

No. 200 Italian Pot and Saucer, Matt Green,

9 in.	per doz.	20.00
13 in.	per doz.	36.00

Catalog #10.

197

Cut Flower Vases and Fern Dishes

These Vases are particularly well-suited to the use of florists because of the large number of different sizes and shapes, and because they are not easily upset. Nos. 1V, 2V, and 3V are also made with holes for electric wiring if desired.

No. 201 Trumpet Vase, Matt Green,
12 in. ....per doz. $20.00
18 in. ....per doz. 40.00
21 in. ....per doz. 80.00

No. 202 Flared Top Vase, Matt Green,
3 x 4½ in. ....per doz. 2.80
4 x 6 in. ....per doz. 4.80
3 x 9 in. ....per doz. 6.00
1½ x 9 in. ....per doz. 7.60
4 x 12 in. ....per doz. 8.00
5½ x 10 in. ....per doz. 9.60
4½ x 15 in. ....per doz. 12.00
5½ x 18 in. ....per doz. 20.00

No. 203 Panel Vase, Matt Green,
Sizes and Prices same as for No. 202

No. 1V Vase, Matt Green, 12 in., per doz. $18.00

No. 2V Vase, Matt Green, 12 in., per doz. $18.00
No. 3V Vase, Matt Green, 12 in., per doz. 18.00

No. 207 Low Flower Bowl, High Feet, Matt Green
7 in. ....per doz. 8.00
8 in. ....per doz. 12.00
9 in. ....per doz. 16.00

No. 208 Fern Dish, Matt Green, with liner,
7 in. ....per doz. 4.80
9 in. ....per doz. 7.20

No. 209 Fern Dish, Matt Green, with liner,
5 in. ....per doz. 4.80
6 in. ....per doz. 7.20
7 in. ....per doz. 9.60
8 in. ....per doz. 12.00

Catalog #10.

198

No. 1

No. 2

Catalog #10.

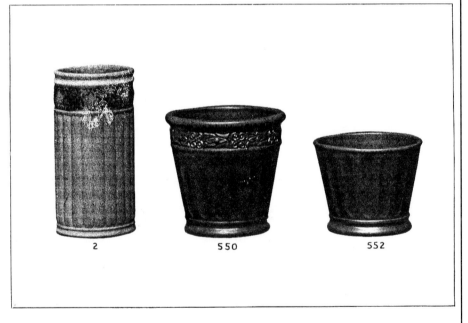

2   550   552

Umbrella and Sand Jars

The items illustrated here, together with Nos. 540 and 550 on Page 23, offer a wide selection of Sand Jars. No. 550, glazed in a beautiful Matt Rose, may be used as a Jardiniere.

No.   1 Umbrella or Sand Jar, Matt Green,
        Bristol White, 10 x 21 in. ....per doz. $40.00
No.   2 Umbrella or Sand Jar, Matt Green,
        Bristol White, 10 x 21 in. ....per doz. 40.00
No.   2 Sand Jar, Stone finish, with green
        decoration, 10 x 21 in. ....per doz. 48.00
No. 550 Jar, Matt Rose and Stone finish, with green
        decoration, 16 in. ....per doz. 60.00
No. 552 Jar, Matt Rose, 11 in. ....per doz. 48.00

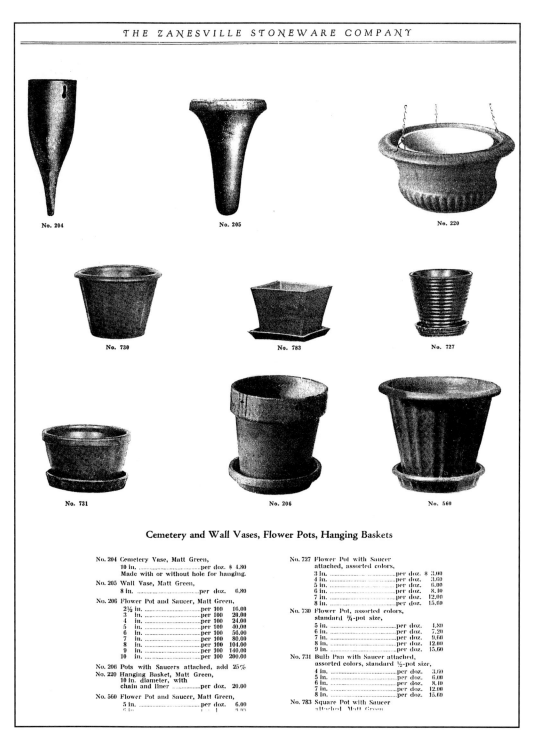

THE ZANESVILLE STONEWARE COMPANY

No. 204

No. 205

No. 220

No. 730

No. 783

No. 727

No. 731

No. 206

No. 560

Cemetery and Wall Vases, Flower Pots, Hanging Baskets

No. 204 Cemetery Vase, Matt Green,
    10 in. ....per doz. $ 4.80
    Made with or without hole for hanging.

No. 205 Wall Vase, Matt Green,
    8 in. ....per doz. 6.80

No. 206 Flower Pot and Saucer, Matt Green,

2½ in.	per 100	16.00
3 in.	per 100	20.00
4 in.	per 100	24.00
5 in.	per 100	40.00
6 in.	per 100	56.00
7 in.	per 100	80.00
8 in.	per 100	104.00
9 in.	per 100	140.00
10 in.	per 100	200.00

No. 206 Pots with Saucers attached, add 25%

No. 220 Hanging Basket, Matt Green,
    10 in. diameter, with
    chain and liner ....per doz. 20.00

No. 560 Flower Pot and Saucer, Matt Green,
    5 in. ....per doz. 6.00
    6 in. ....per doz. 9.00

No. 727 Flower Pot with Saucer
    attached, assorted colors,

3 in.	per doz. $	3.00
4 in.	per doz.	3.60
5 in.	per doz.	6.00
6 in.	per doz.	8.40
7 in.	per doz.	12.00
8 in.	per doz.	15.60

No. 730 Flower Pot, assorted colors,
    standard ¾-pot size,

5 in.	per doz.	4.80
6 in.	per doz.	7.20
7 in.	per doz.	9.60
8 in.	per doz.	12.00
9 in.	per doz.	15.60

No. 731 Bulb Pan with Saucer attached,
    assorted colors, standard ½-pot size,

4 in.	per doz.	3.60
5 in.	per doz.	6.00
6 in.	per doz.	8.40
7 in.	per doz.	12.00
8 in.	per doz.	15.60

No. 783 Square Pot with Saucer
    attached, Matt Green,

Catalog #10.

200

THE ZANESVILLE STONEWARE COMPANY

508   509   510   511   512   513

114   115   515   516   517

Hand-Thrown Ware

Catalog #10.

No. 114 Pitcher, 9 in. ....per doz. $24.00	No. 512 Tray, 3½ in. diameter, per doz. $ 3.00
No. 115 Vase, 9 in. ....per doz. 24.00	No. 513 Vase, 7¾ in. diameter, per doz. 12.00
No. 508 Vase, 6 in. ....per doz. 12.00	No. 515 Pitcher, 9 in. ....per doz. 30.00
No. 509 Vase, 4 in. ....per doz. 6.00	No. 516 Vase, 9 in. ....per doz. 24.00
No. 510 Vase, 4½ in. ....per doz. 4.00	No. 517 Vase, 9 in. ....per doz. 24.00
No. 511 Vase, 3½ in. ....per doz. 3.60	

Colors: Assorted Matt and Gloss

D-11   D-12   518   519

521   522   523   524

Hand-Thrown Ware

201

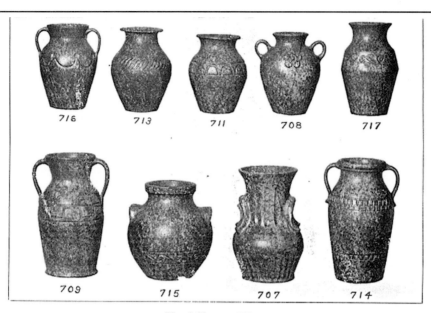

Hand-Thrown Ware

The charm of these lovely hand-thrown shapes is enhanced by the hand-marking and hand-finishing. The finish is a neutral grayish-buff mottled effect like that of the large Oil Jars on Page 20.

No. 707 Vase, 11½ in. ..... per doz. $96.00	No. 711 Vase, 8½ in. ..... per doz. $48.00	No. 715 Vase, 10 in. ..... per doz. $96.00
No. 708 Vase, 9 in. ..... per doz. 60.00	No. 713 Vase, 9 in. ..... per doz. 48.00	No. 716 Vase, 9 in. ..... per doz. 60.00
No. 709 Vase, 12½ in. ..... per doz. 84.00	No. 714 Vase, 12½ in. ..... per doz. 72.00	No. 717 Vase, 10 in. ..... per doz. 60.00

Omar Ware

"Then to the lip of this poor earthen urn
I lean'd, the secret of my life to learn."

Omar Ware is more than a reproduction of ancient pottery; it is a continuation in the present of the art of the past. The wet clay is thumped and batted, the shape is moulded by hand as the wheel turns, in the same manner as that which inspired poets centuries ago. These old shapes, splashed with a dash of color here and there on a dull buff back-ground, preserve the tradition of the potter's art.

765 Vase, 10¼ in. ..... each $9.00	No. 769 Vase, 10 in. ..... each $6.00	No. 773 Vase, 10½ in. ..... each $10.00
766 Vase, 8 in. ..... each 5.00	No. 770 Vase, 8½ in. ..... each 5.00	No. 774 Vase, 9 in. ..... each 8.00
767 Vase, 8¼ in. ..... each 6.00	No. 771 Vase, 10 in. ..... each 7.00	No. 775 Vase, 8 in. ..... each 11.00
768 Vase, 10½ in. ..... each 7.00	No. 772 Vase, 10½ in. ..... each 9.00	No. 776 Vase, 7¾ in. ..... each 5.00

Catalog #10.

Catalog #10.

THE ZANESVILLE STONEWARE COMPANY

792   791   800   757

780   782   777   756   778

Vases and Strawberry Jars

No. 756 Strawberry Jar with
   Saucer attached, 8 in. ....per doz. $30.00
No. 757 Strawberry Pot with
   Saucer attached, 6 in. ....per doz. 18.00
No. 777 Vase, 7½ in. ....per doz. 18.00
No. 778 Jug, 9 in. ....per doz. 18.00

No. 780 Vase, 7½ in. ....per doz. $18.00
No. 782 Vase, 8 in. ....per doz. 18.00
No. 791 Vase, 7 in. ....per doz. 14.40
No. 792 Vase, 6 in. ....per doz. 9.60
No. 792 Vase, 8 in. ....per doz. 11.40
No. 800 Vase, 8 in. ....per doz. 14.40

Colors: Assorted Matt and Gloss

500   799   720   752

577   736   734   737   735

Cooky Jars, Vases, Novelties

No. 500 Hanging Basket, with Chain and Liner,
   7 in. diameter...................per doz. $18.00
No. 577 Vase, 7 in. ....per doz. 8.00

No. 735 Cooky Jar, 8 in. tall.................per doz. $14.40
No. 736 Cooky Jar, 9 in. tall.................per doz. 14.40
No. 737 Cooky Jar with Wicker handle,
   Jar 7½ in. tall ....per doz. 20.40

PLEASE NOTE

The following price changes have been made affecting items illustrated on Pages 10 and 11.

Page 11

No. 26 Vase ....per dozen $ 3.60
No. 27 Vase ....per dozen 3.60
No. 32 Vase ....per dozen 3.60
No. D-23 Vase ....per dozen 7.20

Page 10

No. 500 Hanging Basket .....per dozen $14.40
No. 791 Vase ....per dozen 12.00
No. 792 Vase, 6 in. ....per dozen 8.40
No. 792 Vase, 8 in. ....per dozen 13.20
No. 799 Vase ....per dozen 14.40
No. 800 Vase ....per dozen 12.00

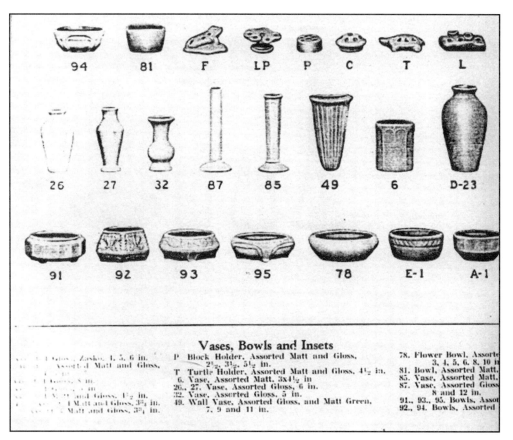

Vases, Bowls and Insets

... Gloss, Zasko, 4, 5, 6 in.	P Block Holder, Assorted Matt and Gloss, 2½, 3½, 5½ in.	78. Flower Bowl, Assorted 3, 4, 5, 6, 8, 10 in
... Assorted Matt and Gloss,	T Turtle Holder, Assorted Matt and Gloss, 4½ in.	81. Bowl, Assorted Matt,
... Gloss, 8 in.	6. Vase, Assorted Matt. 3x4½ in	85. Vase, Assorted Matt.
... Matt and Gloss, 1½ in.	26., 27. Vase, Assorted Gloss, 6 in.	87. Vase, Assorted Gloss 8 and 12 in.
... Matt and Gloss, 3½ in.	32. Vase, Assorted Gloss, 5 in.	91., 93., 95. Bowls, Assor
... Matt and Gloss, 3½ in.	49. Wall Vase, Assorted Gloss, and Matt Green, 7, 9 and 11 in.	92., 94. Bowls, Assorted

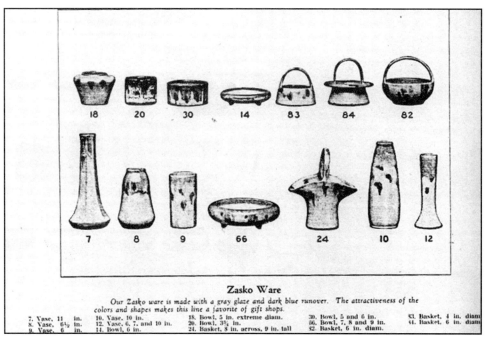

Zasko Ware

Our Zasko ware is made with a gray glaze and dark blue runover. The attractiveness of the colors and shapes makes this line a favorite of gift shops.

7. Vase, 11 in.	10. Vase, 10 in.	18. Bowl, 5 in. extreme diam.	20. Bowl, 5 and 6 in.	83. Basket, 4 in. diam
8. Vase, 6½ in.	12. Vase, 6, 7 and 10 in.	20. Bowl, 3¾ in.	66. Bowl, 7, 8 and 9 in.	84. Basket, 6 in. diam
9. Vase, 6 in.	14. Bowl, 6 in.	24. Basket, 8 in. across, 9 in. tall	82. Basket, 6 in. diam.	

Catalog #10.

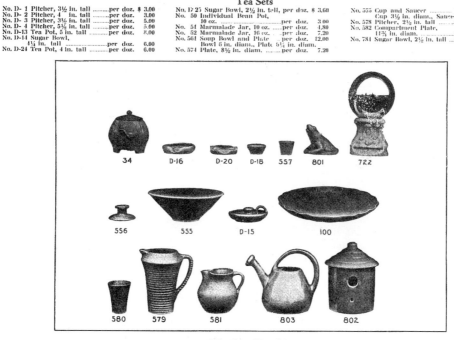

THE ZANESVILLE STONEWARE COMPANY

Tea Sets

No. D- 1 Pitcher, 3½ in. tall ....per doz. $ 3.00
No. D- 2 Pitcher, 4 in. tall ....per doz. 3.00
No. D- 3 Pitcher, 3½ in. tall ....per doz. 5.00
No. D- 4 Pitcher, 5½ in. tall ....per doz. 5.00
No. D-13 Tea Pot, 5 in. tall ....per doz. 8.00
No. D-14 Sugar Bowl,
          4¼ in. tall ....per doz. 6.00
No. D-24 Tea Pot, 4 in. tall ....per doz. 6.00

No. 12 25 Sugar Bowl, 2½ in. tall, per doz. $ 3.60
No. 50 Individual Bean Pot,
          10 oz. ....per doz. 3.00
No. 51 Marmalade Jar, 10 oz. ......per doz. 4.80
No. 52 Marmalade Jar, 16 oz. ......per doz. 7.20
No. 561 Soup Bowl and Plate ...per doz. 12.00
          Bowl 5 in. diam., Plate 6¼ in. diam.
No. 574 Plate, 8½ in. diam. ....per doz. 7.20

No. 575 Cup and Saucer ....per doz. $ 5.80
          Cup 3½ in. diam., Saucer 5¾ in. diam.
No. 578 Pitcher, 2½ in. tall ......per doz. 3.00
No. 582 Compartment Plate,
          11¾ in. diam. ....per doz. 14.45
No. 784 Sugar Bowl, 2½ in. tall ...per doz. 2.40

Gift Shop Novelties

No. D-15 Candlestick, 6 in. diam., per doz. $ 7.20
No. D-16 Ash Tray, 4½ in. diam., per doz. 3.00
No. D-18 Nut Dish, 2¾ in. diam., per doz.   .80
No. D-20 Ash Tray, 4½ in. diam., per doz. 3.00
No. 34 Tobacco Jar, 6 in. tall, per doz. 10.00
No. 100 Lily Pad Bowl, 15 in., per doz. 18.00

No. 555 Bowl, 11 in.,
          Low shape ....per doz. $20.00
No. 556 Candlestick, 4 in. diam., per doz. 4.00
No. 557 Match Holder, 2 in. tall, per doz. 3.60
No. 579 Pitcher, 4 pint ....per doz. 12.00
No. 580 Tumbler 8 oz. ....per doz. 3.00

No. 722 Gazing Globe and Base, 12 in. high.
          Globe, 7 in. Base, 5½ in. Base is
          Mottled Grayish Buff finish, each $ 6.00
No. 801 Frog, 5 in. ....per doz. 7.20
          Made also with closed bottom and slot
          in mouth for child's money bank.

Catalog #10.

789 788 786

813 812 787

Linden Ware

Tea and Chocolate Sets, new in design and color treatment. The pieces are made with Gloss Green under parts and Buff tops.

No. 786 Cream Pitcher, 3½ in. high ....per doz. $ 6.00
No. 787 Chocolate Pot, 10 in. high overall,
    capacity 3 pint ....per doz. 24.00
No. 788 Tea Pot, 5¾ in. high,
    capacity 2 pint ....per doz. 12.00

No. 789 Sugar Bowl, 4½ in. high.............per doz. $7.20
No. 812 Cup and Saucer............................per doz. 9.60
    (Cup, 3½ in. diam.; Saucer, 6 in. diam.)
No. 813 Plate, 9 in. diameter......................per doz. 8.40

805

804

Catalog #10.

806

809

807

Japanese Garden Bowls

Bowls similar to those listed may also be had in special shapes and sizes if desired.

No. 801 Bowl, triangular shape,
    sides 12 in. ....per doz. $30.00
    sides 16 in. ....per doz. 60.00
    sides 20 in. ....per doz. 96.00
No. 805 Bowl, square shape,
    12½ in. x 12½ in. ....per doz. 30.00
    16 in. x 16 in. ....per doz. 60.00
    20 in. x 20 in. ....per doz. 96.00
No. 806 Bowl, rectangular shape,
    8½ in. x 12 in. ....per doz. 30.00
    10 in. x 15 in. ....per doz. 60.00
    12 in. x 18 in. ....per doz. 96.00

No. 807 Bowl, oval shape,
    8½ in. x 11 in. ....per doz. $30.00
    11 in. x 16 in. ....per doz. 60.00
    14 in. x 20 in. ....per doz. 96.00

No. 809 Bowl, round shape,
    9 in. diam. ....per doz. 7.20
    11 in. diam. ....per doz. 12.00
    13 in. diam. ....per doz. 24.00
    16 in. diam. ....per doz. 40.00
    18 in. diam. ....per doz. 72.00

Colors: Assorted Matt and Gloss

No. 811

No. 810

No. 810 Window Box, assorted matt and gloss, 8 in. x 24 in. ....each $ 8.00
No. 811 Mail Box, gloss green, 6 in. x 9 in. ....per doz. 18.00

Catalog #10.

THE ZANESVILLE STONEWARE COMPANY

$\mathcal{W}$E CALL particular attention to the handsome decorative pieces presented on this and the following pages. They include gracefully-shaped hand-thrown Jars, Strawberry Jars small and large, massive Oil Jars and other garden ornaments, every piece of excellent design, beautiful, strong, lasting.

No. 808

No. 808 Sprinkling Pot, assorted matt and gloss colors,
9½ in. high overall ....per doz. $36.00

No. 815 Sprinkling Pot, assorted matt and gloss colors,
8 in. high overall ....per doz. 24.00
(Same shape as No. 808, but with fern design.)

No. 793

No. 793 Sprinkling Pot, assorted matt and gloss colors, 18 in. high overall ....each $8.00

710   721

207

Nos. 558 and 706 make excellent Sand Jars. The Iron Tripod shown with No. 706 will also fit No. 558.

No. 558 Jar, 15 in. tall, opening 10 in. ....each $ 6.00
No. 558 Jar with Iron Stand, height over all, 26 in., each 11.50
No. 705 Jar with Hammered Iron Stand, 30 in. extreme
    height, height of Jar 26 in., opening 6½ in. each 27.00

No. 706 Bowl with Iron Stand, 20½ in. extreme height,
    outside diam. 16½ in., inside diam. 11½ in., each $10.00

Colors: Assorted Matt and Gloss

Catalog #10.

Nos. 751 and 790 may be used either with or without the Iron Tripod in the illustration.

No. 751 Jar, 21 in. tall, opening 6½ in. ....each $12.00
No. 751 Jar with Iron Stand, 30 in. high over all, each 16.00

No. 790 Jar, 17 in. tall by 16 in. extreme diam.,
    opening 7 in. ....each $ 7.00
No. 790 Jar with Iron Stand, 26 in. high over all, each 11.00
No. 798 Jar, 19 in. tall, opening 4½ in. ....each 8.00

Colors: Assorted Matt and Gloss

208

106   118   120

No. 106 Jar, 22 in. tall, opening 8   in. ....each $ 15.00
No. 118 Jar, 21 in tall, opening 5   in. ....each   12.00
No. 120 Jar, 25 in. tall, opening 7½ in. ....each   20.00

Colors: Assorted Matt and Gloss

Catalog #10.

109   112   111

107   110

No. 107 Jar, 26 in. tall, opening 9   in. ....each $ 30.00
No. 110 Jar, 22 in. tall, opening 10½ in. ....each   30.00

Colors: Assorted Matt and Gloss

Catalog #10.

108   119   113

No. 108 Jar, 28 in. tall, opening 11 in. ....each $ 20.00
No. 113 Jar, 32 in. tall, opening 10 in. ....each   25.00
No. 119 Jar, 21 in. tall, opening 7 in. ....each   15.00

Colors: Assorted Matt and Gloss

704   562

No. 562 Jar, 32 in. tall, opening 6½ in. ....each $ 25.00
No. 704 Jar, 23 in. tall, opening 10   in. ....each   25.00

Colors: Assorted Matt and Gloss

Catalog #10.

718   719

No. 719 Jar illustrates a run over glaze, dark blue over light gray. For Jars with this run over glaze, 10 percent extra is charged.

211

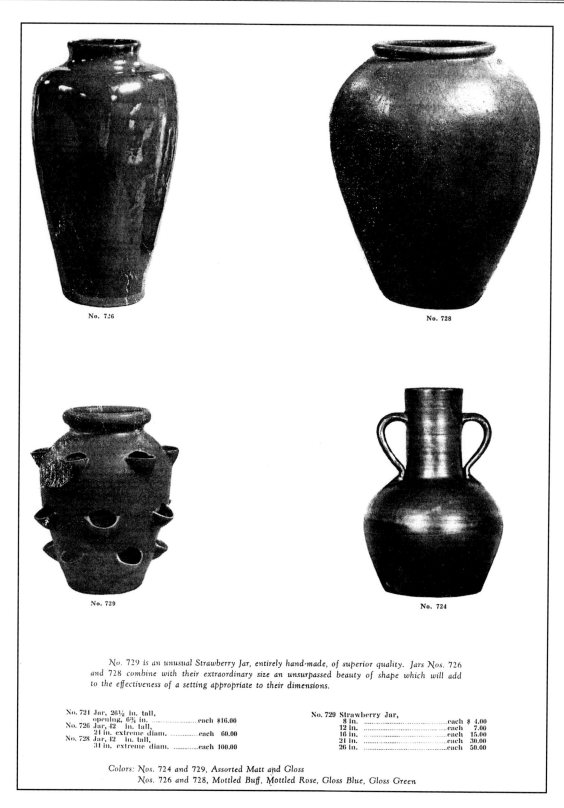

No. 726

No. 728

No. 729

No. 724

No. 729 is an unusual Strawberry Jar, entirely hand-made, of superior quality. Jars Nos. 726 and 728 combine with their extraordinary size an unsurpassed beauty of shape which will add to the effectiveness of a setting appropriate to their dimensions.

No. 724 Jar, 26½ in. tall,
    opening, 6¾ in. ....each $16.00
No. 726 Jar, 42 in. tall,
    24 in. extreme diam. ....each 60.00
No. 728 Jar, 42 in. tall,
    31 in. extreme diam. ....each 100.00

No. 729 Strawberry Jar,
    8 in. ....each $ 4.00
    12 in. ....each 7.00
    16 in. ....each 15.00
    21 in. ....each 30.00
    26 in. ....each 50.00

*Colors: Nos. 724 and 729, Assorted Matt and Gloss
Nos. 726 and 728, Mottled Buff, Mottled Rose, Gloss Blue, Gloss Green*

Catalog #10.

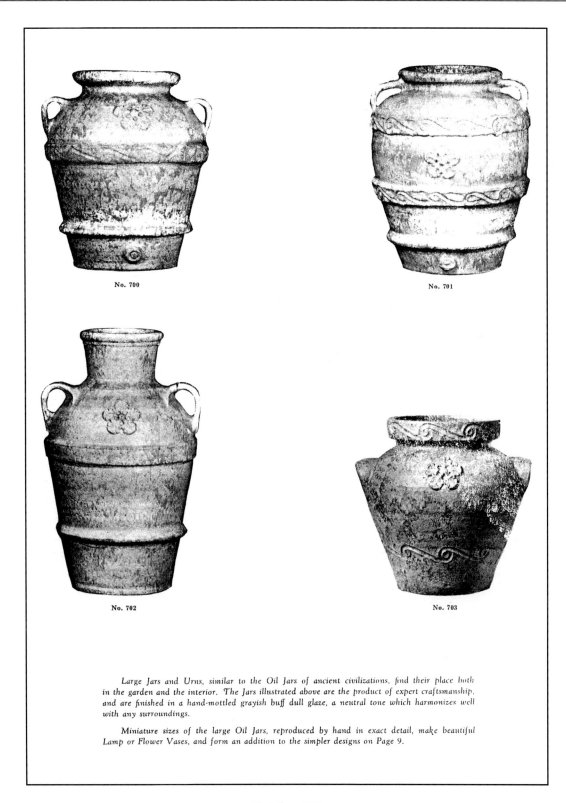

No. 700

No. 701

No. 702

No. 703

Large Jars and Urns, similar to the Oil Jars of ancient civilizations, find their place both in the garden and the interior. The Jars illustrated above are the product of expert craftsmanship, and are finished in a hand-mottled grayish buff dull glaze, a neutral tone which harmonizes well with any surroundings.

Miniature sizes of the large Oil Jars, reproduced by hand in exact detail, make beautiful Lamp or Flower Vases, and form an addition to the simpler designs on Page 9.

Catalog #10.

No. 743

No. 740

No. 742

No. 741

No. 758

Our newest development in garden pottery is this group of Pots. Hand-thrown, hand-finished, and unglazed, they have an artistic roughness and shaded natural color which is most unusual and appealing.

No. 740 Pot, 16 in. high; diam. at top, 17½ in. ....each $12.00
No. 741 Pot, 16½ in. high; diam. at top, 15 in. ....each 12.00
No. 742 Pot, 16 in. high; diam. at top, 19 in. ....each 14.00
No. 743 Pot, 17½ in. high; diam. at top, 18 in. ....each 12.00
No. 758 Pot, 17½ in. high; diam. at top, 16 in. ....each 12.00

Catalog #10.

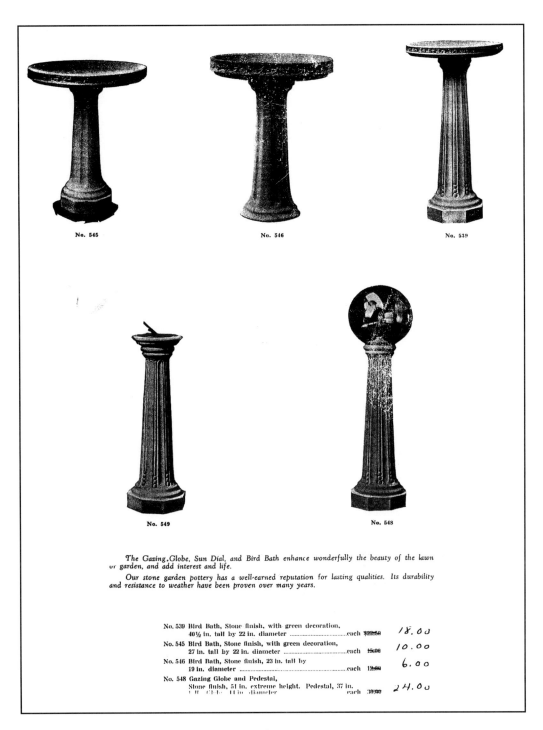

No. 545   No. 546   No. 539

No. 549   No. 548

The Gazing-Globe, Sun Dial, and Bird Bath enhance wonderfully the beauty of the lawn or garden, and add interest and life.

Our stone garden pottery has a well-earned reputation for lasting qualities. Its durability and resistance to weather have been proven over many years.

No. 539 Bird Bath, Stone finish, with green decoration,
    40½ in. tall by 22 in. diameter ....each $22.50   *18.00*

No. 545 Bird Bath, Stone finish, with green decoration,
    27 in. tall by 22 in. diameter ....each 15.00   *10.00*

No. 546 Bird Bath, Stone finish, 23 in. tall by
    19 in. diameter ....each 12.00   *6.00*

No. 548 Gazing Globe and Pedestal,
    Stone finish, 51 in. extreme height. Pedestal, 37 in.
    Glass Globe, 11 in. diameter ....each 30.00   *24.00*

Catalog #10.

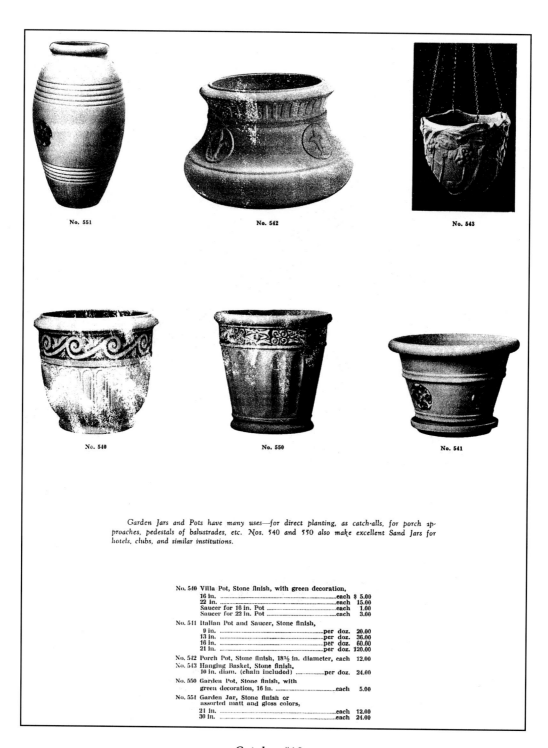

No. 551   No. 542   No. 543

No. 540   No. 550   No. 541

Garden Jars and Pots have many uses—for direct planting, as catch-alls, for porch approaches, pedestals of balustrades, etc. Nos. 540 and 550 also make excellent Sand Jars for hotels, clubs, and similar institutions.

No. 540 Villa Pot, Stone finish, with green decoration,
16 in.	each	$ 5.00
22 in.	each	15.00
Saucer for 16 in. Pot	each	1.00
Saucer for 22 in. Pot	each	3.00

No. 541 Italian Pot and Saucer, Stone finish,
9 in.	per doz.	20.00
13 in.	per doz.	36.00
16 in.	per doz.	60.00
21 in.	per doz.	120.00

No. 542 Porch Pot, Stone finish, 18½ in. diameter, each 12.00
No. 543 Hanging Basket, Stone finish,
10 in. diam. (chain included) ....per doz. 24.00

No. 550 Garden Pot, Stone finish, with
green decoration, 16 in. ....each 5.00

No. 551 Garden Jar, Stone finish or
assorted matt and gloss colors,
21 in.	each	12.00
30 in.	each	24.00

Catalog #10.

216

THE ZANESVILLE STONEWARE COMPANY

Hotel, Kitchen and Utility Ware

No. 20 Octagon Jug, Mahogany, Green, Blue,
white-lined, 2 quart ....per doz. $4.40

No. 21 Jug, Green, Blue, Brown, white-lined,
5 pint ....per doz. 5.00

No. 42 Jug, Green, Blue, white-lined,
½ pint ....per doz. 3.60
1 pint ....per doz. 4.80
3 pint ....per doz. 6.00
5 pint ....per doz. 8.00

No. 43 Growler, Mahogany, Green, Blue,
white-lined, 5 pint ....per doz. 4.40
7 pint ....per doz. 4.80

No. 44 Mug, Assorted Matt and Clear Glaze,
12 oz. ....per doz. 2.50

No. 45 Custard Cup, Blue, white-lined,
3¼ in. ....per doz. 1.00
3⅝ in. ....per doz. 1.20

No. 46 Marmite, Brown and White,
12 oz. ....per doz. 1.50
16 oz. ....per doz. 2.00
24 oz. ....per doz. 2.50
32 oz. ....per doz. 3.31
48 oz. ....per doz. 4.00

No. 47 Covered Butter, White, blue-banded,
2 lb. ....per doz. 3.60
3 lb. ....per doz. 4.40
5 lb. ....per doz. 6.00

No. 48 Bean Pot, Brown and White,
1 quart ....per doz. $3.96
2 quart ....per doz. 4.86
3 quart ....per doz. 6.00
4 quart ....per doz. 7.20
6 quart ....per doz. 9.00

No. 61 Tea Pot, Mahogany, individual, per doz. 3.50

No. 62 Tea Pot, Mahogany, Green, Blue,
2 pint ....per doz. 5.00
3 pint ....per doz. 6.00

No. 63 Cuspidor, Blue, Green, Brown,
7½ in. ....per doz. 4.00

No. 64 Cuspidor, Matt Green, 7 in. .....per doz. 6.00

No. 65 Mixing Bowl, Blue, white-lined,
5 in. ....per doz. 1.56
6 in. ....per doz. 1.80
7 in. ....per doz. 2.16
8 in. ....per doz. 2.88
9 in. ....per doz. 3.60
10 in. ....per doz. 6.00
11 in. ....per doz. 8.40
12 in. ....per doz. 10.80

No. 69 Cooler, white, blue-banded, faucets included,
2 gal. ....each 3.20
3 gal. ....each 3.60
4 gal. ....each 4.00
5 gal. ....each 4.50
6 gal. ....each 5.20
8 gal. ....each 6.00
10 gal. ....each 7.00
12 gal. ....each 8.50

Catalog #10.

Supplement to Catalog No. 10

The Zanesville Stoneware Co.

ZANESVILLE, OHIO

ITEMS which have been recently added to our line are illustrated in this Supplement,—graceful vase shapes, bowls, floor jar and other pieces; and four new tone-tone color effects. All the numbers are available in our full range of gloss and matt colors, including the lighter shades of Blue, Green, Yellow and Pink we are now producing. The two-tone glazes are limited to certain pieces as indicated.

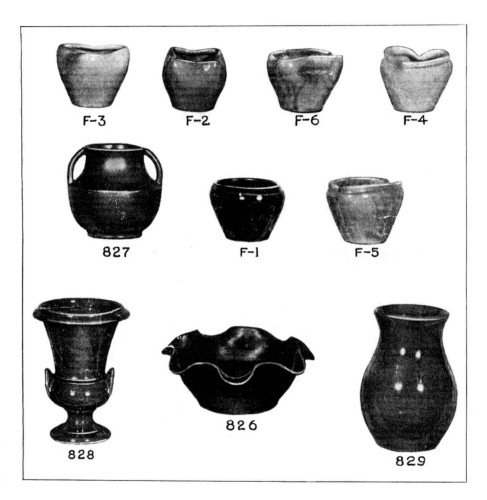

Nos. F-1, F-2, F-3, F-4, F-5 and F-6 Bowls, assorted colors,
    4 inches tall..per dozen $ 3.60
Nos. F-1, F-2, ..., F-4, F-5 and F-6 Bowls, Vulcan Ware
    and Neptune Ware, 4 inches tall.............per dozen 4.80
No. 826 Bowl, assorted colors—
    7 in..per dozen 8.40

8 in..per dozen 9.60
9 in..per dozen 12.00
10 in...per dozen 14.40
No. 827 Vase, assorted colors, 6 in..............per dozen 9.60
No. 828 Vase, assorted colors, 8½ in............per dozen 20.40
No. 829 Vase, assorted colors, 8½ in............per dozen 10.80

Catalog #10.

THE ZANESVILLE STONEWARE COMPANY, ZANESVILLE, OHIO

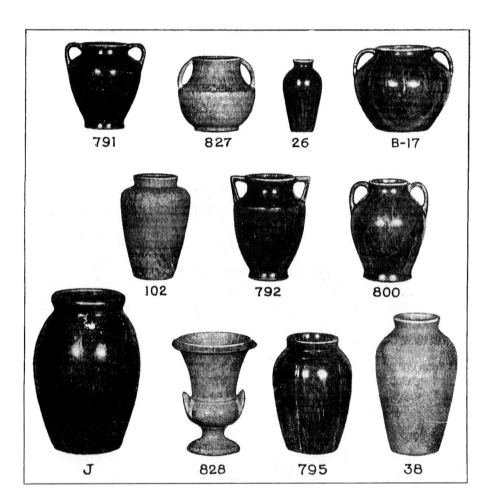

NEPTUNE WARE and VULCAN WARE are a departure from any glazes we have offered in the past. They are rich in color but subdued in tone; in Neptune a dark green predominates, and in Vulcan an orange tint. These glazes are limited to the pieces shown above and to the F series Bowls on the preceding page.

No. B-17	Vase, 7	in.	per dozen	$18.00
No. J	Vase, 12	in.	per dozen	18.00
No. 26	Vase, 6	in.	per dozen	6.00
No. 38	Vase, 10	in.	per dozen	14.40
No. 102	Vase, 8	in.	per dozen	9.60
No. 791	Vase, 7	in.	per dozen	14.40
No. 792	Vase, 8	in.	per dozen	15.60
No. 795	Vase, 8½	in.	per dozen	9.60
No. 800	Vase, 8	in.	per dozen	14.40
No. 827	Vase, 6	in.	per dozen	12.00
No. 828	Vase, 8½	in.	per dozen	24.00

Catalog #10.

THE ZANESVILLE STONEWARE COMPANY, ZANESVILLE, OHIO

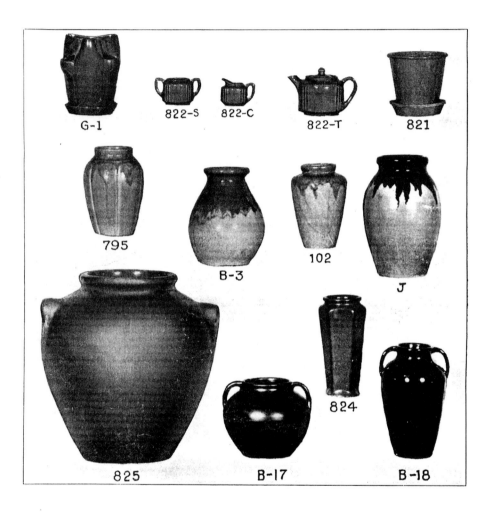

No. B-3 Vase, green over gray, 9½ in. .... per dozen $16.80

No. B-17 Vase, assorted colors, 7 in. .... per dozen 14.40

No. B-18 Vase, assorted colors, 10 in. .... per dozen 14.40

No. G-1 Strawberry Jar with Saucer attached,
      assorted colors, 8 inch .... per dozen 12.00

No. J Vase, assorted colors, 12 inch .... per dozen 14.40

No. J Vase, black over green, 12 inch .... per dozen 16.80

No. 102 Vase, green over gray, 8 inch .... per dozen 9.60

No. 795 Vase, green over gray, 8½ inch .... per dozen 9.60

No. 821 Flower Pot with Saucer attached, assorted colors—
    3 inch .... per dozen $ 3.00
    4 inch .... per dozen 3.60
    5 inch .... per dozen 6.00
    6 inch .... per dozen 8.40
    7 inch .... per dozen 12.00
    8 inch .... per dozen 15.60

No. 822, 3-piece Tea Set, assorted colors .... per dozen 14.40
    Tea Pot .... per dozen 7.20
    Sugar Bowl .... per dozen 4.20
    Cream Pitcher .... per dozen 3.00

No. 821 Vase, assorted colors, 9 inch .... per dozen 7.20

No. 825 Jar, assorted colors, 17 inch .... each 7.00

No. 825 Jar, black over matt green, 17 inch .... each 8.00

Catalog #10.

220

THE ZANESVILLE STONEWARE COMPANY, ZANESVILLE, OHIO

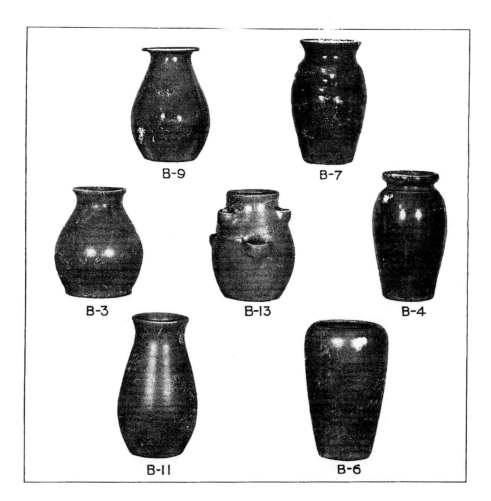

An excellent group of large Vases and Strawberry Jar, priced to retail for as low as $1.00.

No. B-3 Vase, assorted colors, 9   in. .... per dozen $14.40
No. B-4 Vase, assorted colors, 11   in. .... per dozen 14.40
No. B-6 Vase, assorted colors, 10½ in. .... per dozen 14.40

No. B-7 Vase, assorted colors, 11   in. .... per dozen 14.40
No. B-9 Vase, assorted colors, 10   in. .... per dozen 14.40
No. B-11 Vase, assorted colors, 11   in. .... per dozen 14.40
No. B-13 Strawberry Jar, assorted colors, 9 in. ......per dozen 14.40

Catalog #10.

The
Zanesville Stoneware Company

Manufacturers of

Art Ware, Garden Ware
and
High-Grade Glazed
Specialties

Zanesville, Ohio, U. S. A.

Catalog #11.

FOREWORD

$\mathcal{A}$LL THE WARE illustrated in this catalogue is made in a hard-fired body, colored in a variety of glazes. Strength and durability are therefore added to pleasing appearance.

Colors

Plain Colors are Matt Green, Matt Rose, Matt Lavender, Matt Russet, Matt Royal Blue, Gloss Blue, Gloss Green, Gloss Rose, Gloss Black, Gloss Yellow, Seacrest Green, Stardew Blue, Mahogany, and Bristol White. Two-tone and overflow colors are Neptune (Green with rust mottling, gloss finish); Vulcan (a blend in which a reddish tan predominates); Montrose (Rose mottling on Ivory background); Azure (Light Blue with cloudy effect); Brunell (Brown with light splashes and shadings); Forest Green Overflow (Green flow over Russet base); Black flow over Green, Dark Blue flow over light Blue; Zasko (Blue over Gray).

Matt Green Ware

Attention is called to our Matt Green Ware, both Jardinieres, Cut Flower Vases, and so forth, which are produced exclusively in that color, and the various items listed throughout the catalogue which may be ordered in Matt Green. Matt Green is the staple standby which never grows old and is continuous in its appeal to the most refined class of trade.

Hand-thrown Ware

Attention is also directed to our line of genuine hand-made ware, turned up on a potter's wheel. The slightest deviations and irregularities left by the potter's hands give to each piece individuality and beauty.

Pottery for Porch, Lawn, and Garden

Pages 17 to 29 show our pottery for interior and exterior decoration, both in colored glazes and in stone finish. The latter is a rough stone effect which is most attractive and accommodates itself to any surroundings. The large Jars are most reasonably priced, and are available in our full range of colors, including the overflow and two-tone glazes.

Hotel, Kitchen, and Utility Ware

Items of Hotel, Kitchen and Utility Ware are illustrated on Pages 30 and 31. In quality of workmanship and design, we believe these items to be unexcelled by any similar line.

Prices are for goods crated without extra charge,
F.O.B. Zanesville, Ohio

Catalog #11.

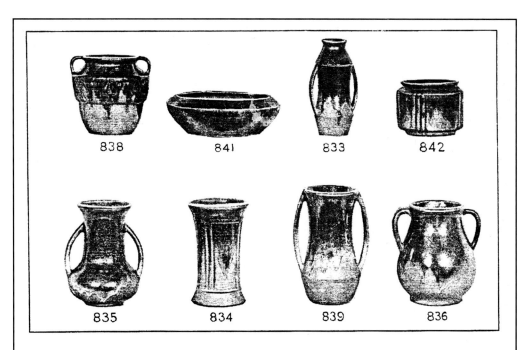

		List for Overflows and Blended Colors		List for Plain Colors, Gloss and Matt
No. 833 Vase, 6¾	in.	per doz. $ 7.20		per doz. $ 6.00
No. 834 Vase, 7	in.	per doz. 9.00		per doz. 7.20
No. 835 Vase, 7	in.	per doz. 10.20		per doz. 9.00
No. 836 Vase, 7	in.	per doz. 14.40		per doz. 12.00
No. 838 Vase, 5¾	in.	per doz. 10.20		per doz. 9.00
No. 839 Vase, 8	in.	per doz. 14.40		per doz. 12.00
No. 841 Bowl, 8	in.	per doz. 12.00		per doz. 10.20
No. 842 Bowl, 5	in.	per doz. 7.20		per doz. 6.00

The numbers shown above and on the opposite page may be obtained both in plain colors, gloss and matt, and in overflow and blended colors. The latter include Forest Green overflow, which is an irregular green over a russet base; Neptune, in which a dark green predominates; Vulcan, showing a dull orange tint; Montrose, with rose mottling on ivory background; Brunell, a rich mahogany grained with lighter shades, Azure, the color of the sky with clouded effect; Black flow over Green base; and Green flow over Gray base.

Catalog #11.

VASES

All sizes suitable for florist or home use.

No. B-18 Vase, 10 in. .... per doz. $11.40
No. 2VH Vase, 12 in. .... per doz. 19.20
No. 301 Vase, 12 in. .... per doz. 16.80
No. 307 Vase, 8½ in. .... per doz. 9.60
No. 308 Vase, 6 in. .... per doz. 4.80

No. 824 Vase, 9 in. .... per doz. 7.20
No. 829 Vase, 8½ in. .... per doz. 9.60
No. 830 Vase, 5 in. .... per doz. 3.60
  8½ in. .... per doz. 7.20
No. 837 Vase, 8½ in. .... per doz. 7.20

Colors: Assorted Matt and Gloss

Catalog #11.

225

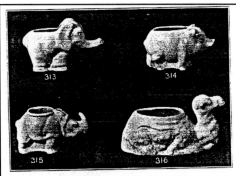

ANIMAL NOVELTIES

No. 313 Elephant, 5¾ in. long.........................per doz. $3.60
No. 314 Pig, 5¼ in. long...............................per doz. 3.60
No. 315 Rhinoceros, 5¼ in. long.......................per doz. 3.60
No. 316 Camel, 6¼ in. long............................per doz. 3.60
             7¼ in. long.............................per doz. 6.00

Colors: Assorted Matt and Gloss

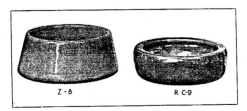

DOG DISHES

No. RC-9 Dog Dish, 7 in..............................per doz. $6.00
No. Z-8 Dog Dish, 6 in...............................per doz. 4.00
              8 in...................................per doz. 8.00

Colors: Gloss Green, Gloss Blue, Gloss Yellow,
White

No. 43-B Pitcher, 6-pint.............................per doz. $4.80
No. 43-S Stein, 16-oz................................per doz. 2.00
Colors: Green, Brown, white-lined

No. C-1 Casserole, 7½ in.............................per doz. $6.00
              9½ in..................................per doz. 12.00
Colors: Green, Blue, Brown, white-lined

Catalog #11.

The
Zanesville Stoneware Company

Manufacturers of

Art Ware, Garden Ware
and
High-Grade Glazed
Specialties

Catalog #12.

THE QUALITY of the ware illustrated in this catalogue has been tested by time and use. A hard-fired body and a variety of colored glazes are joined to add strength, durability and dependability to pleasing appearance.

COLORS are Matt Green, Matt Rose, Matt Lavender, Matt Russet, Royal Matt Blue, Gloss Blue, Gloss Green, Gloss Rose, Gloss Yellow, Royal Gloss Blue, Seacrest Green, Stardew Blue, Pink, Mahogany, Black, White, Neptune (Green with rust mottling), Vulcan (a blend in which a reddish tan predominates), Azure (Light Blue with cloudy effect), Brunell (Brown with light splashes and shadings), Forest Green (Green flow over Russet base), R----rcy (Black flow over light Green), Vorosa (Rose flow over Ivory), Zasko (Dark Blue flow over Gray), Verdantone (Green flow over Gray base), Blumoro (a Moorish Blue tone), Ruddiglow (Red tone with light shading), Ebonello (Yellow flow over Black), and Ebonivor (Black flow over White).

PRICES are F. O. B. Zanesville, Ohio.

Zanesville, Ohio, U. S. A.

227

No. 4 Vase, 8 in.
Matt Green, Seacrest Green, Gloss
Blue, Gloss Rose, White, Black.
Per doz......................$7.20

No. 105 Vase, 7 in.
Matt Green, Seacrest Green, Gloss
Blue, Mahogany, White, Black.
Per doz......................$7.20

No. 834 Vase, 7 in.
Gloss Green, Gloss Blue, White,
Black, Yellow, Matt Russet.
Per doz......................$7.20
Forest Green, Vulcan, Neptune.
Per doz......................$9.00

No. 576 Vase, 8½ in.
Gloss Green, Gloss Blue, White,
Black, Yellow, Matt Lavender.
Per doz......................$7.20

No. 795 Vase, 8½ in.
Gloss Green, Gloss Blue, Gloss Rose,
Black, Yellow, Royal Matt Blue.
Per doz......................$7.20
Neptune, Vulcan. Per doz..... 9.00

No. 837 Vase, 8½ in.
Matt Green, Seacrest Green, Gloss
Blue, White, Gloss Rose, Black.
Per doz......................$7.20
Ebonello, Azure, Brunell.
Per doz......................$9.00

No. 829 Vase, 8½ in.
Seacrest Green, Yellow, Stardew
Blue, Matt Rose, Mahogany, White.
Per doz......................$7.20

No. 830 Vase, 5 in.
Matt Green, Gloss Blue, Seacrest
Green, White, Stardew Blue, Matt
Rose. Per doz................$3.60
Ebonello, Verdantone, Blumoro,
Ruddiglow. Per doz..........$4.20

8 in.
Matt Green, Gloss Blue, Seacrest
Green, White, Stardew Blue, Matt
Rose. Per doz................$7.20
Ebonello, Verdantone, Blumoro,
Ruddiglow. Per doz..........$9.00

No. 858 Vase, 6 in.
Gloss Green, Gloss Blue, White,
Yellow, Black, Seacrest Green.
Per doz......................$6.00
Verdantone, Blumoro, Ruddiglow.
Per doz......................$7.20

No. 335 Vase, 8 in.
Gloss Green, Gloss Blue, White,
Black, Seacrest Green, Yellow.
Per doz......................$7.20

No. 26 Vase, 6 in.
Black, White, Gloss Rose, Seacrest
Green, Gloss Blue, Yellow.
Per doz......................$3.60
Blumoro, Ruddiglow, Verdantone,
Vulcan. Per doz.............$4.20

No. 27 Vase, 6 in.
Mahogany, Matt Rose, Matt Green,
White, Royal Matt Blue, Matt
Lavender. Per doz......$3.60
Vorosa, Bacorcy. Per doz.....$4.20

No. 32 Vase, 5 in.
Gloss Green, Matt Russet, Yellow,
Gloss Rose, Black. Per doz.....$3.60

No. 318 Vase, 6½ in.
Seacrest Green, Stardew Blue, Yellow, White, Black, Gloss Blue.
Per doz......................$6.00

Catalog #12.

228

No. 37 Vase, 12 in.
Matt Green, Seacrest Green, Gloss
Blue, Black, Matt Rose, Royal Matt
Blue, Pink. Per doz.........$14.40
Ebonello. Per doz..........$18.00

No. B-7 Vase, 11 in.
Seacrest Green, Gloss Blue, Gloss
Green, White, Gloss Rose, Pink,
Stardew Blue. Per doz......$14.40

No. B-4 Vase, 11 in.
Seacrest Green, Gloss Green, Gloss
Blue, White, Black, Yellow.
Per doz.....................$14.40

No. B-6 Vase, 10½ in.
Gloss Green, Seacrest Green, Gloss
Blue, White, Black, Gloss Rose,
Yellow. Per doz.............$14.40

No. 330 Vase
Gloss Green, Seacrest Green, Gloss
Blue, Gloss Rose, Black, White,
Yellow, Stardew Blue.
6 in. Per doz..............$ 4.50
8 in. Per doz..............$ 7.20
10 in. Per doz..............$12.00

No. 577 Vase
Matt Green, Gloss Green, Seacrest
Green, Gloss Blue, Pink, Black,
White, Yellow.
5½ in. Per doz..............$ 3.60
7 in. Per doz..............$ 6.00
10 in. Per doz..............$10.80
11 in. Per doz..............$14.40

No. 307 Vase, 8½ in.
Gloss Green, Gloss Blue, Yellow,
Black, Gloss Rose, White.
Per doz.....................$9.60
Ebonello, Azure, Brunell.
Per doz.....................$12.00

No. 38 Vase, 10 in.
Gloss Blue, Seacrest Green, Matt
Lavender, White, Black, Mahogany.
Per doz.....................$12.00

No. B-11 Vase, 11 in.
Matt Russet, Matt Green, Matt Rose,
Seacrest Green, Gloss Blue, Yellow.
Per doz.....................$14.40

No. J Vase, 12 in.
Gloss Green, Gloss Blue, Gloss Rose,
Black, White, Seacrest Green, Royal
Matt Blue. Per doz..........$14.40
Neptune, Vulcan, Forest Green.
Per doz.....................$18.00

Catalog #12.

229

No. 800 Vase, 8 in.
Seacrest Green, Gloss Blue, Matt
Rose, White, Royal Matt Blue,
Mahogany. Per doz....$12.00
Neptune, Vulcan, Brunell, Azure.
Per doz......................$14.40

No. 792 Vase, 6 in.
Seacrest Green, Stardew Blue, Pink,
White, Black, Yellow. Per doz.,$6.00

8 in.
Matt Green, Seacrest Green, Gloss
Blue, Gloss Rose, Black, White.
Per doz......................$13.20
Neptune, Vulcan, Vorosa, Baccroy.
Per doz......................$15.60

No. 836 Vase, 7 in.
Gloss Green, Matt Russet, White,
Black, Gloss Rose, Stardew Blue.
Per doz......................$12.00
Ebonello, Neptune, Vulcan, Forest
Green. Per doz............$14.40

No. 791 Vase, 7 in.
Black, Seacrest Green, Yellow, Matt
Lavender, Royal Matt Blue, White.
Per doz.....................,$12.00
Ebonello, Neptune, Vulcan, Azure.
Per doz......................$14.40

No. 839 Vase, 8 in.
White, Black, Matt Green, Seacrest
Green, Yellow, Royal Matt Blue.
Per doz......................$12.00
Biumoro, Verdantone, Ruddiglow,
Forest Green. Per doz.......$14.40

No. 780 Vase, 7½ in.
Mahogany, Gloss Green, Stardew
Blue, Pink, Matt Lavender, Black.
Per doz......................$12.00

No. 851 Vase, 8x8 in.
Gloss Green, Seacrest Green, Gloss
Blue, White, Black, Gloss Rose.
Per doz......................$12.00
Ebonello, Brunell, Azure, Neptune.
Per doz......................$14.40

No. 828 Vase, 8½ in.
Seacrest Green, Stardew Blue, Yel-
low, White, Black, Pink.
Per doz......................$18.00
Verdantone, Biumoro, Ruddiglow,
Neptune. Per doz...........$20.40

No. 838 Vase, 5¾ in.
Stardew Blue, Gloss Rose, Seacrest
Green, White, Black, Yellow.
Per doz......................$9.60
Forest Green, Vorosa, Baccroy,
Azure. Per doz......$10.00

No. 835 Vase, 7 in.
White, Black, Gloss Blue, Seacrest
Green, Matt Lavender, Mahogany.
Per doz......................$9.60
Biumoro, Ruddiglow, Verdantone,
Forest Green. Per doz........$12.00

No. 827 Vase, 6 in.
Yellow, Matt Rose, White, Seacrest
Green, Black, Royal Matt Blue.
Per doz......................$9.60
Biumoro, Ruddiglow, Verdantone,
Vulcan. Per doz............$12.00

No. B-17 Vase, 6 in.
Seacrest Green, White, Black, Pink,
Yellow, Gloss Blue. Per doz...$9.60
Ebonello, Brunell, Azure.
Per doz......................$12.00

8 in.
Matt Green, Seacrest Green, White,
Black, Gloss Rose, Gloss Blue.
Per doz......................$14.40
Ebonello, Neptune, Vulcan, Forest
Green. Per doz............$18.00

Catalog #12.

230

No. 201 Trumpet Vase
Matt Green, Black, White, Seacrest
Green, Gloss Blue, Gloss Rose,
Yellow.
12 in. Per doz............$14.40
18 in. Per doz............ 28.80
24 in. Per doz............ 57.60

No. 202 Flared Top Vase
Matt Green, Black, White, Seacrest
Green, Stardew Blue, Gloss Rose.
3x4½ in. Per doz..........$ 2.80
4x6   in. Per doz.......... 4.80
3x9   in. Per doz.......... 6.00
4½x9 in. Per doz.......... 7.60
4x12 in. Per doz.......... 8.00
5½x10 in. Per doz.......... 9.60
4½x15 in. Per doz.......... 12.00
5½x18 in. Per doz.......... 20.00

No. 203 Panel Vase
Matt Green, Black, White, Gloss
Blue, Gloss Green, Yellow.
Sizes and prices same as No. 202
Vase.

No. 2V Vase, 12 in.
Matt Green, Royal Matt Blue, White,
Matt Lavender, Black, Gloss Rose.
Per doz.....................$18.00

No. B-18 Vase, 10 in.
Stardew Blue, Yellow, Pink, Matt
Green, Black, White. Per doz..$14.40

No. 3V Vase, 12 in.
Gloss Green, Gloss Blue, Seacrest
Green, White, Mahogany, Matt Rose.
Per doz.....................$18.00

No. 2VH Vase, 12 in.
Seacrest Green, Gloss Blue, Gloss
Rose, Black, White, Yellow, Matt
Green, Mahogany. Per doz...$19.20
Ebonello, Forest Green, Neptune,
Vulcan. Per doz............$24.00

No. 301 Vase, 12 in.
Mahogany, Black, Gloss Blue, Matt
Rose, Seacrest Green, Royal Matt
Blue. Per doz...............$16.80

No. 4VH Vase, 12 in.
Gloss Green, Gloss Blue, Black,
White, Yellow, Pink, Seacrest Green,
Royal Matt Blue. Per doz....$19.20
Biumaro, Ruddiglow, Verdantone.
Per doz.....................$24.00

Catalog #12.

No. D-12 Pitcher
Matt Green, Seacrest Green, Gloss
Blue, Yellow, Mahogany,
Gloss Rose.
2-qt. Per doz...............$18.00
4-qt. Per doz............... 24.00
8-qt. Per doz............... 36.00

No. 114 Pitcher, 5-pt.
Matt Green, Matt Rose, Royal Matt
Blue, White, Seacrest Green, Black.
Per doz....................$24.00

No. D-11 Pitcher, 2-qt.
Gloss Green, Gloss Blue, Yellow,
Matt Lavender, Matt Green, Matt
Russet. Per doz.............$18.00

No. 516 Vase, 9 in.
Gloss Green, Gloss Blue, Gloss Rose,
Black, Yellow, Mahogany.
Per doz.....................$24.00

No. 515 Pitcher, 5-pt.
Gloss Green, Gloss Blue, Gloss Rose,
Black, Yellow, Matt Lavender.
Per doz....................$30.00

No. 517 Vase, 9 in.
Matt Green, Seacrest Green, White,
Stardew Blue, Pink, Black, Blumoro,
Verdantone, Ruddiglow.
Per doz.....................$24.00

No. 521 Vase, 12 in.
White, Black, Gloss Green, Gloss
Blue, Gloss Rose, Matt Green,
Vorosa, Bacorcy. Per doz.....$36.00

No. 519 Vase, 9 in.
Matt Rose, Royal Matt Blue, White,
Matt Lavender, Black, Matt Green.
Per doz....................$18.00

No. 518 Vase, 8 in.
Seacrest Green, Stardew Blue, Pink,
Yellow, White, Gloss Blue.
Per doz.....................$18.00

No. 523 Vase, 9 in.
Gloss Green, Gloss Blue, Gloss Rose,
White, Black, Yellow. Per doz..$24.00

Hand-Thrown Ware
The pieces illustrated above are
examples of the true Potter's art,
that of shaping by hand on the
turning wheel. The slight deviations and impressions left by the
potter's hands give to each piece
individuality and beauty that
moulded pieces do not have.

Catalog #12.

No. F-12 Hanging Strawberry Pot with Chain, 5 in.
Seacrest Green, Gloss Blue, Gloss Rose, Black, White, Stardew Blue, Yellow, Gloss Green, Pink.
Per doz........................$7.20

No. 500 Hanging Basket with Chain and Liner, 7 in.
Matt Green, Gloss Blue, Gloss Rose, Matt Lavender, Black, Royal Matt Blue. Per doz...............$14.40

No. 220 Hanging Basket with Chain and Liner, 10 in.
Matt Green, Seacrest Green, Royal Matt Blue, Matt Rose, Black, White.
Per doz.....................$20.00

No. 803 Sprinkling Pot, 9" high over all
Gloss Green, Yellow, Gloss Blue, Seacrest Green, Gloss Rose.
Per doz.....................$30.00

No. 205 Wall Vase, 8 in.
Matt Green, Gloss Blue, Seacrest Green. Yellow, Black, Gloss Rose.
Per doz........................$6.80

No. 331 Hanging Basket with Chain, 6¼ in.
Gloss Green, Gloss Blue, Black, Pink, White, Seacrest Green, Gloss Rose, Yellow, Stardew Blue.
Per doz........................$9.60

No. 24 Basket, 8" wide x 9" high
Gloss Green, Gloss Blue, White, Black, Matt Lavender, Gloss Rose.
Per doz.......................$12.00
Verosa, Bacossy. Per doz....14.40

No. 204 Cemetery Vase, 10 in.
Matt Green (made with or without hole for hanging). Per doz....$4.80

No. 328H Basket, 7" wide x 8½" high
Matt Green, Royal Matt Blue, Pink, Seacrest Green, Yellow, White, Black, Gloss Blue. Per doz....$12.00

No. 323 Basket, 3½" wide x 5½" high
White, Yellow, Black, Gloss Blue, Gloss Rose, Seacrest Green.
Per doz........................$2.40

No. F-14 Basket, 6" wide x 8½" high
Gloss Green, Gloss Blue, Seacrest Green, Stardew Blue, Yellow, Black Gloss Rose, White. Per doz....$6.00

No. F-17 Basket, 8" wide x 9" high
Seacrest Green, Stardew Blue, Pink, White, Black, Yellow. Per doz..$14.40
Verdantone, Blumoro, Ruddiglow.
Per doz.....................$18.00

Catalog #12.

233

**No. 850 Flower Pot
with Saucer Attached**
Matt Green, Gloss Green, Seacrest
Green, Gloss Blue, Gloss Rose, Pink,
Yellow, Black, White, Royal Matt
Blue, Matt Lavender.
3 in. Per doz..............$ 3.00
4 in. Per doz.............. 3.60
5 in. Per doz.............. 6.00
6 in. Per doz.............. 8.40
7 in. Per doz.............. 12.00
8 in. Per doz.............. 15.60

**No. 840 Flower Pot
with Saucer Attached**
Matt Green, Gloss Green, Seacrest
Green, Gloss Blue, Gloss Rose, Matt
Russet, Yellow, Black, White, Matt
Rose, Stardew Blue.
Same sizes and prices as No. 850.

No. 560 Flower Pot and Saucer
Matt Green, Gloss Green, Seacrest
Green, Gloss Blue, Gloss Rose,
Yellow, Black, White, Royal Matt
Blue.
5 in. Per doz..............$ 6.00
6 in. Per doz.............. 9.00
7 in. Per doz.............. 12.00
8 in. Per doz.............. 15.00
9 in. Per doz.............. 19.20
10 in. Per doz.............. 24.00

**No. 857 Flower Pot,
Standard ¾-Pot Size**
Matt Green, Gloss Green, Seacrest
Green, Gloss Blue, Gloss Rose,
Yellow, Black, White, Stardew Blue,
Pink.
5 in. Per doz..............$ 4.80
6 in. Per doz.............. 7.20
7 in. Per Doz.............. 9.60
8 in. Per doz.............. 12.00
9 in. Per doz.............. 15.60

No. 856 Flower Pot
Matt Green, Gloss Green, Seacrest
Green, Gloss Blue, Stardew Blue,
Gloss Rose, Yellow, Black, White,
Pink.
5 in. Per doz..............$ 4.80
6 in. Per doz.............. 7.20
7 in. Per doz.............. 9.60
8 in. Per doz.............. 12.00
9 in. Per doz.............. 15.60

**No. 730 Flower Pot,
Standard ¾-Pot Size**
Matt Green, Gloss Green, Seacrest
Green, Gloss Blue, Yellow, Black,
Gloss Rose, White, Royal Matt Blue.
Same sizes and prices as No. 857.

**No. 852 Flower Pot with Saucer
Attached, Standard ½-Pot Size**
Matt Green, Gloss Green, Seacrest
Green, Gloss Blue, Yellow, Black,
Gloss Rose, White, Matt Russet,
Pink, Stardew Blue.
5 in. Per doz..............$ 6.00
6 in. Per doz.............. 8.40
7 in. Per doz.............. 12.00
8 in. Per doz.............. 15.60

**No. 731 Flower Pot with Saucer
Attached, Standard ½-Pot Size**
Matt Green, Gloss Green, Seacrest
Green, Gloss Blue, Yellow, Black,
Gloss Rose, White, Matt Rose, Matt
Lavender, Royal Matt Blue.
4 in. Per doz..............$ 3.60
5 in. Per doz.............. 6.00
6 in. Per doz.............. 8.40
7 in. Per doz.............. 12.00
8 in. Per doz.............. 15.60
10 in. Per doz.............. 24.00
13 in. Per doz.............. 40.00
16 in. Per doz.............. 57.60

**No. 783 Square Pot
with Saucer Attached**
Matt Green, Gloss Green, Seacrest
Green, Gloss Blue, Gloss Rose, Pink,
Yellow, Black, White, Royal Matt
Blue, Stardew Blue.
4 in. Per doz.............. $5.40
5 in. Per doz.............. 9.00
4 in. Pot only. Per doz...... 3.60
5 in. Pot only. Per doz...... 6.00

No. 206 Flower Pot and Saucer
Matt Green, Gloss Green, Seacrest
Green Gloss Blue, Yellow, Black,
Gloss Rose, White, Stardew Blue,
Pink.
2½ in. Per doz..............$ 2.40
3 in. Per doz.............. 3.00
4 in. Per doz.............. 3.60
5 in. Per doz.............. 6.00
6 in. Per doz.............. 8.40
7 in. Per doz.............. 12.00
8 in. Per doz.............. 15.60
9 in. Per doz.............. 19.20
10 in. Per doz.............. 24.00

Catalog #12.

234

No. 328 Bowl
Seacrest Green, Gloss Blue, White,
Black, Pink, Yellow.
6 in. Per doz.............$ 7.20
8 in. Per doz............. 14.40

No. 328V Bowl with Vase inset, 8 in.
Gloss Green, Gloss Blue, White,
Black, Matt Lavender, Seacrest
Green, Yellow. Per doz.......$18.00

No. 317 Bowl, 8 in.
Seacrest Green, Gloss Blue, White,
Black, Yellow, Gloss Rose.
Per doz.....................$12.00
Verdantone, Blumoro, Ruddiglow.
Per doz.....................$14.40

No. 309 Jardiniere, 7 in.
White, Black, Gloss Blue, Seacrest
Green, Stardew Blue, Yellow, Gloss
Rose, Matt Green. Per doz.....$7.20

No. 845 Jardiniere, 7½"
Seacrest Green, Yellow, Gloss Blue,
White, Black, Gloss Rose.
Per doz.....................$7.20

No. 752 Tulip-shaped Jardiniere, 7"
White, Black, Gloss Rose, Yellow,
Gloss Green, Gloss Blue, Matt
Green. Per doz.......$7.20

**No. 729 Strawberry Jar
with Saucer Attached**
Matt Green, Seacrest Green, Yellow,
Black, White, Gloss Rose, Gloss
Blue, Gloss Green, Forest Green.
5 in. Per doz.............$ 7.20
8 in. Per doz............. 18.00
10 in. Per doz............. 36.00

No. B-13 Strawberry Jar, 9 in.
Gloss Green, Gloss Blue, Black,
White, Yellow, Gloss Rose.
Per doz.....................$14.40

No. BA-12 Pig, 6" long
White, Yellow, Gloss Blue, Seacrest
Green, Pink, Matt Lavender.
Per doz.....................$3.60

No. BA-13 Duck, 5¼" long
White, Yellow, Gloss Blue, Seacrest
Green, Pink, Royal Matt Blue.
Per doz.....................$3.60

No. BA-14 Elephant, 5½" long
White, Yellow, Gloss Blue, Pink,
Seacrest Green, Mahogany.
Per doz.....................$3.60

No. 313 Elephant, 5¾" long
Seacrest Green, Stardew Blue, Gloss
Rose, White, Yellow, Black, Gloss
Green. Per doz.............$3.60

No. 314 Pig, 5⅛" long
Seacrest Green, Stardew Blue, Gloss
Rose, White, Yellow, Black, Gloss
Green. Per doz.............$3.60

No. 315 Rhinoceros, 5⅛" long
Seacrest Green, Stardew Blue, Gloss
Rose, White, Yellow, Black.
Per doz.....................$3.60

No. 316 Camel
Seacrest Green, Stardew Blue, Gloss
Rose, White, Yellow, Black, Matt
Russet.
6¼" long. Per doz...........$3.60
7⅛" long. Per doz........... 6.00

Catalog #12.

No. 25 Jardiniere
Matt Green, Gloss Blue, Seacrest
Green, White, Black.
5 in. Per doz..............$ 3.60
6 in. Per doz.............. 4.80
7 in. Per doz.............. 7.20
8 in. Per doz.............. 12.00
9 in. Per doz.............. 18.00
10 in. Per doz.............. 24.00

No. 322 Jardiniere
Gloss Green, Gloss Blue, Gloss Rose,
Black, White, Yellow, Mahogany,
Matt Russet.
5 in. Per doz..............$ 3.60
6 in. Per doz.............. 4.80
7 in. Per doz.............. 7.20
8 in. Per doz.............. 10.80

No. 0 Jardiniere
Matt Green, Seacrest Green, Gloss
Green, Gloss Blue, White, Black,
Gloss Rose, Yellow.
3 in. Per doz..............$ 2.40
4 in. Per doz.............. 2.40
5 in. Per doz.............. 3.00
6 in. Per doz.............. 3.60
7 in. Per doz.............. 6.00
8 in. Per doz.............. 11.00
9 in. Per doz.............. 13.00
10 in. Per doz.............. 16.00
12 in. Per doz.............. 30.00

No. 22 Jardiniere and Pedestal
Matt Green, Gloss Blue, Seacrest
Green, Gloss Rose, Ebonello, Forest
Green.
9 in. Jard., 16 in. Ped. Each..$4.00
10 in. Jard., 20 in. Ped. Each.. 6.00

No. 332 Jardiniere
Seacrest Green, Stardew Blue, Matt
Green, White, Black, Pink, Royal
Matt Blue, Yellow.
5 in. Per doz..............$ 3.60
6 in. Per doz.............. 4.80
7 in. Per doz.............. 7.20
8 in. Per doz.............. 10.80
10 in. Per doz.............. 19.20

No. 23 Jardiniere and Pedestal
Gloss Green, Gloss Blue, Yellow,
Black, Brunell, Bacorcy, Verdantone.
9 in. Jard., 16 in. Ped. Each..$4.00
10 in. Jard., 20 in. Ped. Each.. 6.00

Catalog #12.

236

No. 804 Bowl, Triangular Shape
Matt Green, Black, White, Gloss
Blue.
Sides 9 in. Per doz.........$14.40
Sides 12 in. Per doz.......... 30.00
Sides 16 in. Per doz.......... 60.00
Sides 20 in. Per doz......... 96.00

No. 805 Bowl, Square Shape
Gloss Green, Stardew Blue, Gloss
Rose, Yellow.
9"x 9". Per doz.......$14.40
12½"x12½". Per doz....... 30.00
16"x 16". Per doz....... 60.00
20"x 20". Per doz....... 96.00

No. 809 Bowl, Round Shape
Matt Green, Gloss Blue, White, Gloss
Green, Gloss Rose, Black, Yellow.
 9 in. Per doz..............$ 7.20
11 in. Por doz.............. 12.00
13 in. Per doz.............. 24.00
16 in. Per doz.............. 40.00
18 in. Per doz.............. 72.00

No. 806 Bowl, Rectangular Shape
Seacrest Green, Stardew Blue, Pink,
Yellow, White, Black.
 6"x10". Per doz..........$14.40
8½"x12". Per doz.......... 30.00
10"x15". Per doz.......... 60.00
12"x18". Per doz.......... 96.00

No. 807 Bowl, Oval Shape
Gloss Green, Gloss Blue, Gloss Rose,
White, Black, Royal Matt Blue, Matt
Green.
 6"x11". Per doz...........$14.40
8½"x14". Per doz........... 30.00
11"x16". Per doz........... 60.00
14"x20". Per doz........... 96.00

No. 801 Frog, 5 in.
Matt Green. Per doz.........$7.20

No. 100 Lily Pad Bowl, 15 in.
White, Black, Yellow, Gloss Blue,
Seacrest Green, Pink, Gloss Green,
Matt Green, Stardew Blue, Royal
Matt Blue, Matt Lavender.
Per doz......................$48.00

No. 843 Bowl with Base, 8 in.
Matt Rose, Gloss Blue, Black, White,
Seacrest Green. Per doz......$18.00

No. 826 Bowl
Seacrest Green, Gloss Green, Gloss
Blue, Stardew Blue, Yellow, Pink,
White, Black.
 7 in. Per doz..............$ 8.40
 8 in. Per doz.............. 9.60
 9 in. Per doz.............. 12.00
10 in. Per doz.............. 14.40

No. 832 Bowl, 8 in.
Royal Matt Blue, White, Black, Matt
Green, Seacrest Green, Gloss Rose.
Per doz......................$12.00

No. 841 Bowl, 8 in.
Gloss Green, Gloss Blue, Yellow,
Gloss Rose, White, Black.
Per doz......................$10.20
Vorosa, Bacorcy, Forest Green.
Per doz......................$12.00

No. 556 Candlestick
4 in. Diam. Per doz..........$4.00
Colors to match Nos. 100 and 555
Bowls.

No. 555 Bowl, 11 in.
White, Black, Seacrest Green, Gloss
Blue, Royal Matt Blue, Pink, Yellow.
Per doz......................$24.00

No. F Frog Flower Holder
4½ in. Per doz..............$8.00
Colors to match any bowls.

No. LP Lily Pad Flower Holder
3¾ in. Per doz..............$8.00
Colors to match any bowls.

No. C Crown Flower Holder
2½". Per doz................$2.40
3½". Per doz................ 3.60
4". Per doz................ 6.00
5". Per doz................ 9.00
Colors to match any bowls.

No. 207 Bowl, with Feet
Mat Lavender, Matt Rose, Royal
Matt Blue, Matt Green, White, Black,
Yellow.
7 in. Per doz..............$ 8.00
8 in. Per doz.............. 12.00
9 in. Per doz.............. 16.00

Catalog #12.

No. F-1 Bowl, 4" high
Seacrest Green, Stardew Blue, Pink,
Yellow, White, Matt Russet.
Per doz..........................$3.60
Forest Green, Ebonello.
Per doz.......................$4.80

No. F-2 Bowl, 4" high
Matt Green, Gloss Green, Black,
Gloss Blue, Gloss Rose, Royal Matt
Blue. Per doz................$3.60
Neptune, Vulcan. Per doz.....$4.80

No. F-3 Bowl, 4" high
Colors and prices same as No. F-1.

No. F-4 Bowl, 4" high
Colors and prices same as No. F-2.

No. F-5 Bowl, 4" high
Colors and prices same as No. F-1.

No. F-6 Bowl, 4" high
Colors and prices same as No. F-2.

No. BA-1 Bowl
Seacrest Green, Gloss Green, Gloss
Blue, Yellow, Pink, Black, White,
Royal Matt Blue.
6 in. Per doz.................$6.00
8 in. Per doz.................12.00
8 in. Ebonello. Per doz.......$14.40

No. BA-2 Bowl, 6 in.
Gloss Green, Stardew Blue, Gloss
Rose, Black, White, Matt Green.
Per doz.......................$4.80

No. BA-3 Bowl, 6 in.
Gloss Blue, Seacrest Green, Yellow,
White, Black, Pink. Per doz....$3.60

No. BA-10 Bowl, 6 in.
Yellow, Mahogany, Seacrest Green,
White, Gloss Blue, Pink.
Per doz.......................$4.80

No. 78 Bowl
Matt Green, Seacrest Green, White,
Black, Yellow, Gloss Blue, Gloss
Rose.
3 in. Per doz..............$ 3.00
4 in. Per doz.............. 3.50
5 in. Per doz.............. 4.00
6 in. Per doz.............. 4.80
8 in. Per doz.............. 10.00
10 in. Per doz.............. 16.00

No. 91 Bowl, 6 in.
Stardew Blue, Gloss Green, Gloss
Rose, White, Royal Matt Blue, Matt
Russet. Per doz..............$3.60

No. BA-6 Bowl, 5 in.
Gloss Green, Stardew Blue, Gloss
Rose, Mahogany, Matt Green, Matt
Russet.
Per doz.......................$2.40

No. BA-8 Bowl, 5 in.
White, Seacrest Green, Yellow Matt
Green, Black, Royal Matt Blue.
Per doz.......................$2.40

No. BA-11 Bowl, 5 in.
Gloss Blue, White, Yellow, Pink,
Seacrest Green, Matt Lavender.
Per doz.......................$2.40

No. 305 Bowl, 5 in.
Seacrest Green, Gloss Blue, Yellow,
White, Black, Gloss Rose.
Per doz.......................$6.00

No. S-5 Bowl, 5½ in.
Seacrest Green, Gloss Blue, Yellow,
Black, White, Gloss Rose.
Per doz.......................$5.00

No. BA-4 Bowl, 5 in.
Gloss Green, Gloss Blue, Yellow,
Pink, White, Black. Per doz...$3.60

No. 511 Vase, 3½ in.
Seacrest Green, Gloss Blue, Pink,
Yellow, White, Black. Per doz., $3.60

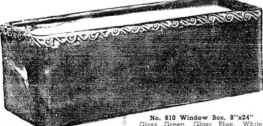

No. 810 Window Box, 8"x24"
Gloss Green, Gloss Blue, White,
Black, Yellow, Seacrest Green.
Each.........................$6.00

No. 303 Window Box, 12 in.
Seacrest Green, Gloss Green, White,
Black, Gloss Blue, Yellow, Gloss
Rose, Royal Matt Blue.
Per doz.......................$18.00

Catalog #12.

No. 579 Pitcher, 4-pt.
Seacrest Green, Gloss Blue, Gloss
Rose, Black, Gloss Green, Yellow.
Per doz.....................$12.00

No. 580 Tumbler, 8 oz.
Colors to match No. 579.
Per doz......................$2.40

No. D-27 Bowl, 5 in.
Seacrest Green, White, Black, Pink,
Yellow, Gloss Blue, Stardew Blue,
Gloss Rose, Gloss Green, Mahogany.
Per doz.....................$2.40

No. D-26 Pitcher, 5 in. high
Seacrest Green, Gloss Blue, White,
Pink, Yellow, Mahogany.
Per doz.....................$3.60

No. 581 Pitcher, 3-pt.
Matt Green, Matt Rose, Seacrest
Green, Yellow, Gloss Blue, Royal
Matt Blue. Per doz...........$12.00

No. 52 Marmalade Jar, 16 oz.
Seacrest Green, Gloss Blue, Gloss
Rose, Yellow. Per doz........$7.20

No. D-1 Pitcher, 3½" high
Seacrest Green, Gloss Blue, Yellow,
Gloss Rose, Mahogany, Royal Matt
Blue, Matt Green. Per doz.....$3.00

No. D-2 Pitcher, 4" high
Seacrest Green, Gloss Blue, Yellow,
Pink, White, Black, Stardew Blue.
Gloss Green. Per doz........$3.00

No. D-4 Pitcher, 5½" tall
Royal Matt Blue, Matt Rose, Matt
Lavender, Matt Russet, Matt Green,
Black. Per doz..............$5.00

No. 401 Pitcher, 3 in.
Seacrest Green, Stardew Blue, Pink,
Yellow, White, Mahogany, Matt
Green. Per doz........$3.00

No. 402 Sugar Bowl, 2½" high
Colors to match No. 401.
Per doz.....................$3.00

No. F-10 Ash Tray, 4 in.
Seacrest Green, Gloss Blue, White,
Black, Yellow, Gloss Rose.
Per doz.....................$2.00

No. F-13 Ash Tray, 4 in.
Gloss Green, Stardew Blue, White,
Black, Yellow, Pink. Per doz...$2.00

No. D-16 Ash Tray, 4½ in.
Matt Green, Royal Matt Blue, Matt
Rose, Matt Russet, Mahogany,
Black. Per doz. $3.00

No. D-20 Ash Tray, 4½ in.
Seacrest Green, Gloss Blue, Yellow,
Pink, White, Stardew Blue.
Per doz.....................$3.00

No. D-18 Nut Dish, 2¾ in.
Matt Green, Seacrest Green, Gloss
Rose, Yellow, Gloss Blue, White,
Black. Per doz...............$0.80

No. 557 Match Holder, 2" high
Matt Green, Seacrest Green, Yellow,
Gloss Rose, Gloss Blue, White,
Black. Per doz..............$2.40

No. D-15 Candlestick, 6" diam.
Matt Green, Matt Rose, Yellow,
Black, Seacrest Green, Gloss Blue.
Per doz.....................$7.20

No. 34 Tobacco Jar 6" high
Mahogany, Gloss Blue, Gloss Green,
Gloss Rose, Black, Yellow.
Per doz.....................$10.00

No. F-7 Cigarette Box, 4¼ in.
Seacrest Green, Gloss Blue, Yellow,
Black, White, Gloss Rose.
Per doz.....................$6.00

No. 311 Window Box,
4¼"x15", depth 4¼"
Seacrest Green, Gloss Green, Gloss
Blue, White, Black, Yellow, Gloss
Rose. Per doz..............$24.00

No. 312 Window Pot,
4¼"x5", depth 5¾"
Same colors as No. 311. Per doz..$7.20
Nos. 311 and 312 may be arranged
in several different combinations
to make up Window Boxes of any
length.

No. F-18 Cowboy Hat Ash Tray, 6½"
Gloss Blue, Seacrest Green, Gloss
Rose, Yellow, White, Black.
Per doz...:..................$3.00

Catalog #12.

No. D-3 Pitcher, 3½" high
Colors to match No. D-13.
Per doz.......................$5.00

No. D-14 Sugar Bowl, 4¼" high
Colors to match No. D-13.
Per doz.......................$6.00

No. D-13 Tea Pot, 4-cup
Matt Green, Gloss Blue, Yellow,
Gloss Rose, Mahogany, Seacrest
Green, Matt Lavender.
Per doz.......................$8.00

No. D-24 Tea Pot, 2-cup
Gloss Green, Gloss Blue, Black, Matt
Lavender, Gloss Rose, Yellow,
Seacrest Green. Per doz.......$6.00

No. 578 Pitcher, 2½" high
Colors to match No. D-24.
Per doz.......................$3.00

No. 784 Sugar Bowl, 2½" high
Colors to match No. D-24.
Per doz.......................$2.40

No. 822-C Pitcher, 2½" high
Colors to match No. 822-T.
Per doz.......................$3.00

No. 822-S Sugar Bowl, 2½" high
Colors to match No. 822-T.
Per doz.......................$4.20

No. 822-T Tea Pot, 4-cup
Gloss Green, Seacrest Green, Pink,
Stardew Blue, Mahogany, Black,
White. Per doz...............$7.20

No. 575 Cup and Saucer
Cup 3½" diam., Saucer 5¾" diam.
Seacrest Green, Gloss Blue, Gloss
Rose, Yellow, Matt Green,
Mahogany. Per doz..........$9.00

No. 574 Plate, 8½" diam.
Colors to match No. 575.
Per doz.......................$7.20

No. 561 Soup Bowl and Plate
Bowl 6" diam., Plate 6¼" diam.
Colors to match No. 575.
Per doz.......................$12.00

LINDEN WARE
Tea and Chocolate Sets in two
color treatments, Gloss Green under
parts with Buff tops and Royal Blue
under parts with Buff tops.

No. 786 Pitcher, 3½" high
Per doz.......................$6.00

No. 789 Sugar Bowl, 4½" high
Per doz.......................$7.20

No. 788 Tea Pot, 4-cup
Per doz.......................$12.00

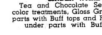

No. 787 Chocolate Pot, 10" high, 3-pt.
Per doz.......................$24.00

No. 813 Plate, 9" diam.
Per doz.......................$8.40

No. 812 Cup and Saucer
Cup 3½" diam., Saucer 6" diam.
Per doz.......................$9.60

Catalog #12.

240

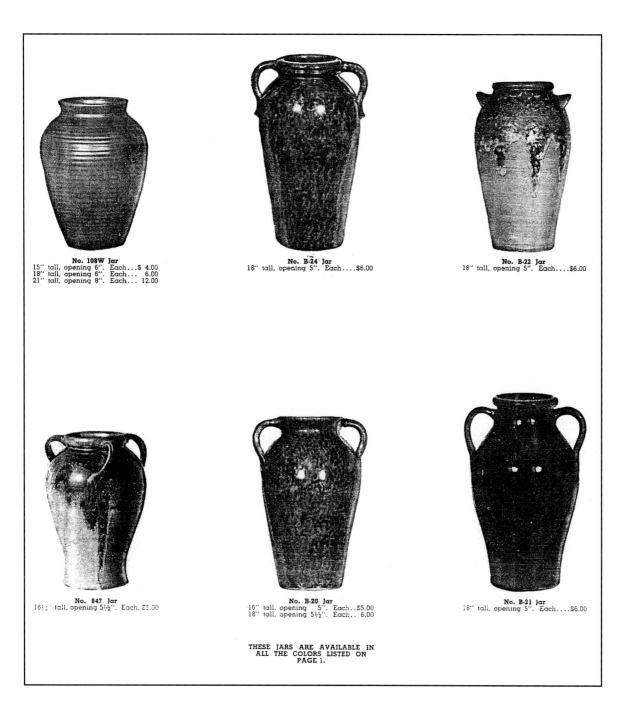

No. 108W Jar
15" tall, opening 6". Each...$ 4.00
18" tall, opening 6". Each... 6.00
21" tall, opening 8". Each... 12.00

No. B-24 Jar
18" tall, opening 5". Each....$6.00

No. B-22 Jar
18" tall, opening 5". Each....$6.00

No. 847 Jar
16½" tall, opening 5½". Each. $5.00

No. B-20 Jar
16" tall, opening 5". Each..$5.00
18" tall, opening 5½". Each.. 6.00

No. B-21 Jar
18" tall, opening 5". Each....$6.00

THESE JARS ARE AVAILABLE IN
ALL THE COLORS LISTED ON
PAGE 1.

Catalog #12.

No. 844 Jar
18″ tall, opening 4½″. Each..$6.00

No. 855 Jar
12″ tall, opening 5″. Each....$5.00

No. 848 Jar
22″ to top of handles, opening 5¼″.
Each.......................$7.00

No. 825 Jar
With Iron Stand, 22″ high overall.
Each.........................$10.00
Jar only, 16½″ tall, opening 8″.
Each.........................$7.00
Iron Stand only. Each........$4.00

No. 859 Jar
18″ tall, opening 6½″. Each...$7.00

No. 790 Jar
17″ tall, opening 7″. Each....$7.00
With Iron Stand, 26″ high overall.
Each.......................$11.00

THESE JARS ARE AVAILABLE IN
ALL THE COLORS LISTED ON
PAGE 1.

Catalog #12.

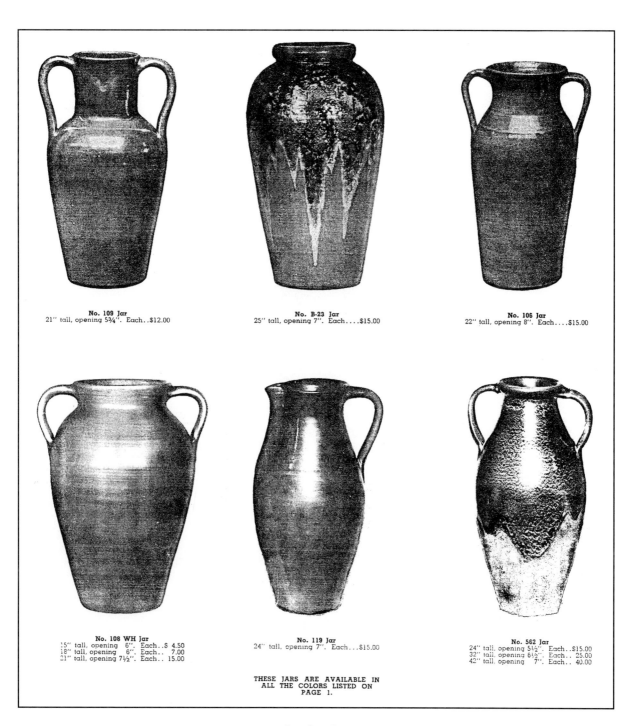

No. 109 Jar
21" tall, opening 5¾". Each..$12.00

No. B-23 Jar
25" tall, opening 7". Each....$15.00

No. 106 Jar
22" tall, opening 8". Each....$15.00

No. 108 WH Jar
15" tall, opening 6". Each..$ 4.50
18" tall, opening 6". Each.. 7.00
21" tall, opening 7½". Each.. 15.00

No. 119 Jar
24" tall, opening 7". Each...$15.00

No. 562 Jar
24" tall, opening 5½". Each..$15.00
32" tall, opening 6½". Each.. 25.00
42" tall, opening 7". Each.. 40.00

THESE JARS ARE AVAILABLE IN
ALL THE COLORS LISTED ON
PAGE 1.

Catalog #12.

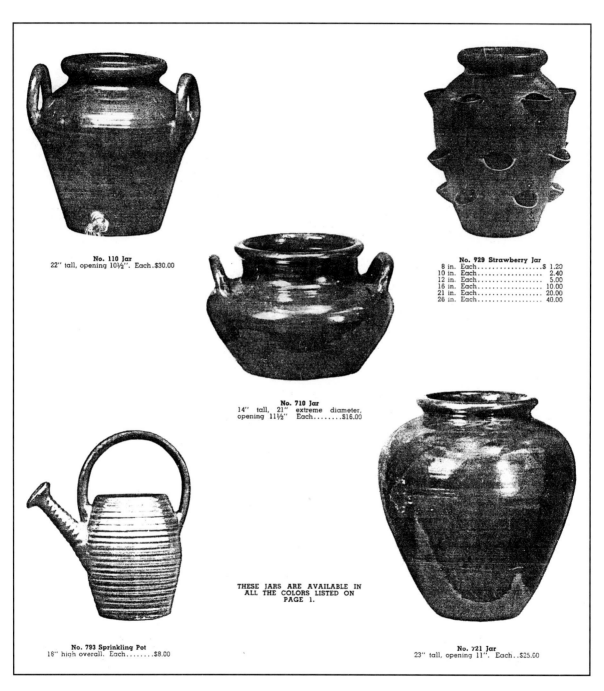

No. 110 Jar
22" tall, opening 10½". Each.$30.00

No. 729 Strawberry Jar

8 in.	Each	$ 1.20
10 in.	Each	2.40
12 in.	Each	5.00
16 in.	Each	10.00
21 in.	Each	20.00
26 in.	Each	40.00

No. 710 Jar
14" tall, 21" extreme diameter,
opening 11½" Each........$16.00

THESE JARS ARE AVAILABLE IN
ALL THE COLORS LISTED ON
PAGE 1.

No. 793 Sprinkling Pot
18" high overall. Each........$8.00

No. 721 Jar
23" tall, opening 11". Each..$25.00

Catalog #12.

No. 718 Jar
26" tall, opening 10". Each..$25.00

No. 719 Jar
27" tall, opening 10½". Each.$20.00

No. 551 Jar
24" tall, opening 7". Each..$12.00
30" tall, opening 8½". Each.. 24.00

No. 113 Jar
32" tall, opening 10". Each..$25.00

THESE JARS ARE AVAILABLE IN
ALL THE COLORS LISTED ON
PAGE 1.

No. 108 Jar
27" tall, opening 11". Each..$20.00

Catalog #12.

No. 701 Oil Jar
26 in. tall. Each.............$50.00

No. 725 Jar
35 in. tall. Each.............$40.00

No. 702 Oil Jar
33 in. tall. Each.............$50.00

No. 728 Jar
42 in. tall, 34 in. extreme diameter.
Each.....................$100.00

THESE JARS ARE AVAILABLE IN
ALL THE COLORS LISTED ON
PAGE 1.

No. 705 Jar
With Iron Stand, 30 in. extreme
height, height of Jar 26 in., opening
9 in. Each................$27.00

Catalog #12.

246

No. 1 Umbrella or Sand Jar
10 x 21 in.
Matt Green, White. Per doz...$40.00

No. 2 Umbrella or Sand Jar
10 x 21 in.
Matt Green, White, Gloss Blue, Matt Rose, Black. Per doz........$40.00
Stone finish with Green decoration. Per doz.....................$48.00

No. 552 Jar, 14" tall
Matt Green, White, Royal Matt Blue, Matt Russet. Per doz........$48.00

No. 558 Jar, 15" tall, opening 10"
Matt Green, Gloss Green, Black, Gloss Blue, Gloss Rose, Yellow, Neptune. Each..............$6.00
With No. 706 Iron Stand, 26" height overall. Each..............$11.50

No. 550 Jar, 16" tall
Gloss Green, Gloss Blue, Gloss Rose, White, Stone finish with Green decoration. Per doz.........$60.00

No. 540 Villa Pot, 16" top diameter
Gloss Green, Seacrest Green, Gloss Blue, Yellow, Gloss Rose, Stone finish with Green decoration, White with Green decoration, White with Blue decoration, White with Rose decoration, Yellow with Black decoration, Mottled Buff with Green decoration. Each.............$5.00
22" top diameter, Stone finish with Green decoration. Each......$15.00
Saucer for 16" Villa Pot. Each.$1.00
Saucer for 22" Villa Pot. Each.$3.00

No. 553 Porch Pot, 13" top diameter
Stone finish. Per doz........$24.00
Gloss Green, Seacrest Green, Matt Green, Gloss Blue, Yellow, Gloss Rose, Black, White, Royal Matt Blue. Per doz.....................$30.00

16" top diameter, Stone finish. Per doz.....................$42.00
Gloss Green, Seacrest Green, Matt Green, Gloss Blue, Yellow, Gloss Rose, Black, White, Royal Matt Blue. Per doz.....................$48.00

13" Pot with Pedestal, 23½" height overall. Stone finish. Per doz..$42.00
Gloss Green, Seacrest Green, Matt Green, Gloss Blue, Yellow, Gloss Rose, Black, White, Royal Matt Blue. Per doz.....................$48.00

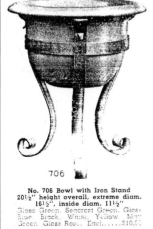

706

No. 706 Bowl with Iron Stand
20½" height overall, extreme diam. 16½", inside diam. 11½"
Gloss Green, Seacrest Green, Gloss Blue, Black, White, Yellow, Matt Green, Gloss Rose. Each......$10.00

Catalog #12.

No. 541 Italian Pot and Saucer
Stone finish, Matt Green, Gloss
Green, Seacrest Green, Yellow,
Gloss Blue, White.
9 in. Per doz..............$ 20.00
13 in. Per doz.............. 36.00
16 in. Per doz.............. 60.00
21 in. Per doz.............. 120.00

No. 543 Hanging Basket
Stone finish, 10'' diameter, (Chain
included). Per doz...........$24.00

**No. 548 Gazing Globe and Pedestal,
Stone Finish**
Pedestal 37'' tall, Globe 14'' diam.,
51'' overall. Each...........$24.00
Pedestal 24'' tall, Globe 10'' diam.,
34'' overall. Each...........$10.00

**No. 549 Sun Dial and Pedestal,
Stone Finish**
42'' extreme height, Dial 9¼'' diam.
Each.......................$22.00
29'' extreme height, Dial 7'' diam.
Each.......................$10.00

No. 545 Bird Bath
Stone finish with Green trim, 27''
tall by 22' diam. Each........$6.00

No. 546 Bird Bath
Stone finish, Natural Buff with Green
trim on top and pedestal, 23'' tall
by 19'' diameter. Each........$3.00

No. 539 Bird Bath
Stone finish, 40½'' tall by 22'' diam.
Each.......................$15.00

**No. 538 Bird Bath
26'' tall by 19'' diameter**
Stone finish.............each, $4.00
Gloss Green, Gloss Blue, Gloss Rose.
White.................each, $6.00

Catalog #12.

No. H-1 Dog Dish, 6" wide x 3" deep
Gloss Green, Gloss Blue, Gloss Rose,
Yellow. Per doz..............$4.80

No. H-2 Dog Dish, 7" wide x 4" deep
Gloss Green, Gloss Blue, Gloss Rose,
Yellow. Per doz..............$7.20

No. F-15 Dog Dish
Seacrest Green, Stardew Blue, Gloss
Rose, Yellow.
6 in. Per doz..............$4.00
7 in. Per doz.............. 6.00

No. F-16 Water Dish
Seacrest Green, Stardew Blue, Gloss
Rose, Yellow.
6 in. Per doz..............$4.00
7 in. Per doz.............. 6.00

No. Z-8 Dog Dish
Gloss Green, Gloss Blue, Yellow,
Gloss Rose.
6 in. Per doz..............$4.00
8 in. Per doz.............. 8.00

No. RC-9 Dog Dish, 7 in.
Gloss Green, Gloss Blue, Yellow,
Gloss Rose. Per doz..........$6.00

No. 735 Cooky Jar, 8" tall
Gloss Green, Gloss Blue, Mahogany,
Yellow, Gloss Rose, Black.
Per doz.....................$14.40

No. 736 Cooky Jar, 9" tall
Seacrest Green, Stardew Blue,
Mahogany, Yellow, White.
Per doz.....................$14.40

No. 56 Casserole, 6 in.
Yellow, with lower half Brown.
Per doz.....................$4.80

No. 57 Ramekin, 4½ in.
Yellow, with lower half Brown.
Per doz.....................$3.00

No. 45 Custard Cup
Gloss Green, Gloss Blue, Gloss Rose,
Yellow, Mahogany.
3¼ in. Per doz..............$1.00
3¾ in. Per doz.............. 1.20

No. 46 Marmite
White, with lower half Brown.
4 oz. Per doz..............$1.60
8 oz. Per doz.............. 1.80
12 oz. Per doz.............. 2.00
16 oz. Per doz.............. 2.50
24 oz. Per doz.............. 2.88
32 oz. Per doz.............. 3.34
48 oz. Per doz.............. 4.00

No. 48 Bean Pot
Brown, with lower half White.
1 qt. Per doz..............$3.96
2 qt. Per doz.............. 4.86
3 qt. Per doz.............. 6.00
4 qt. Per doz.............. 7.20
5 qt. Per doz.............. 9.00

No. C-1 Casserole
Gloss Green, Gloss Blue, Yellow,
Mahogany, all white-lined.
7½ in. Per doz..............$ 6.00
9½ in. Per doz.............. 12.00

No. C-2 Casserole, 7½"
Gloss Blue, Gloss Green, Yellow,
Mahogany, all white-lined.
Per doz.....................$6.00

No. 65 Mixing Bowl
Blue, white-lined.
5 in. Per doz..............$ 1.56
6 in. Per doz.............. 1.80
7 in. Per doz.............. 2.16
8 in. Per doz.............. 2.88
9 in. Per doz.............. 3.60
10 in. Per doz.............. 6.00
11 in. Per doz.............. 8.40
12 in. Per doz.............. 10.80

Catalog #12.

249

No. 61 Tea Pot, Individual
Mahogany. Per doz..........$3.50

No. 62 Tea Pot
Mahogany, Gloss Green, Gloss Blue.
2 pt. Per doz.................$5.00
3 pt. Per doz................. 6.00

No. 63 Cuspidor, 7½ in.
Gloss Green, Gloss Blue, Mahogany,
Black. Per doz...............$4.00

No. 64 Cuspidor, 7 in.
Matt Green, Matt Rose, Royal Matt
Blue. Per doz.................$6.00

No. 47 Covered Butter
White, with Blue Bands.
2 lb. Per doz.................$3.60
3 lb. Per doz................. 4.40
5 lb. Per doz................. 6.00

No. 44 Mug
Gloss Green, Gloss Blue, Mahogany,
Yellow, all white-lined.
10 oz. Per doz.................$2.00
12 oz. Per doz................. 2.00

No. 43-S Stein, 16 oz.
Gloss Green, Mahogany, white-lined.
Per doz......................$2.00

No. 43-B Pitcher, 6-pint
Gloss Green, Mahogany, white-lined
Per doz......................$4.80

No. 43 Pitcher
Gloss Green, Gloss Blue, Mahogany,
all white-lined.
5 pt. Per doz.................$4.40
7 pt. Per doz................. 4.80

No. 21 Pitcher, 6 pint
Gloss Green, Gloss Blue, Mahogany,
all white-lined. Per doz.......$5.00

No. 69 Cooler, Faucet included
White with Blue Bands.
2 gal. Each.................$3.20
3 gal. Each................. 3.60
4 gal. Each................. 4.00
5 gal. Each................. 4.50
6 gal. Each................. 5.20
8 gal. Each................. 6.00
10 gal. Each................. 7.00
12 gal. Each................. 8.50

STONE WATER FILTER
Our Filter has been fully tested
and its merits established as pos-
sessing every practical adaptation
for family use, rendering the most
impure and foul rain, river, or
hydrant water free from all organic
matter, gases, taste or smell. The
process of filtering is shown in the
cut. The water percolates through
a porous stone from the upper to
the lower jar simply by the force
of gravity.

No. 1 Filter, 5 qt.
Capacity per day 2 to 3 gallons.
Each.........................$6.00

No. 2 Filter, 9 qt.
Capacity per day 3 to 5 gallons.
Each.........................$7.00

No. 3 Filter, 12 qt.
Capacity per day 4 to 8 gallons.
Each.........................$8.40

No. 4 Filter, 16 qt.
Capacity per day 6 to 10 gallons.
Each.........................$10.00

No. 6 Filter, 24 qt.
Capacity per day 10 to 14 gallons.
Each.........................$12.00

Special discount will be quoted on
quantity lots.

Made in plain White, or White with
Blue Bands.

Catalog #12.

SUPPLEMENT
to
CATALOGUE NO. 12

No. 585 Urn, 14 in.
Glazed colors. Per doz........$42.00
Stone Finish. Per doz......... 30.00

No. 585 Urn with Pedestal,
24½ in. high overall
Glazed colors. Per doz........$60.00
Stone Finish. Per doz........ 48.00

No. 849 Jar, 16½ in.
Gray with Blue Grapes and Russet
with Burgundy Grapes.
Each $12.00

No. 717 Jar, 20 in.
Glazed colors. Each..........$10.00

Catalog #12 supplement.

No. F-26 Pup, 7½" long
Per doz......................$6.00
Colors: All White, with Blue collar,
Red tongue, and Black eyes
and nose.

No. F-25 Cat, 6½" long
Per doz......................$3.60
Colors: Seacrest Green, Stardew
Blue, Yellow, White. All with Black
eyes, mouth, and whiskers.

No. F-27 Dog and Hamper, 4¼" long
Per doz......................$3.60
Colors: Seacrest Green, Stardew
Blue, Yellow, White. All with
Red eyes and nose.

No. F-28 Boy at Well, 4" high
Per doz......................$3.60
Colors: Seacrest Green, Stardew
Blue, Yellow, White, Pink.

No. F-24 Dutch Shoe, 7½" long
Per doz......................$3.60
Colors: Seacrest Green, Stardew
Blue, Yellow, White, Pink, Black.

No. F-30 Baby Shoe, 4" long
Per doz......................$2.40
Colors: Stardew Blue, Pink,
Seacrest Green, White, Yellow.

No. F-23 Dutch Girl, 8½" high
Per doz......................$12.00
Colors: All White with cap, apron,
and shoes trimmed in Red, Blue
Yellow, and Green.

No. F-31 Bear, 6" long
Per doz......................$3.60
Colors: White, Black, Brown,
Yellow, Seacrest Green,
Gloss Blue.

Nos. J-1, J-3, J-4, J-5, J-9 and
J-10 Jugs, 2 oz.
Per doz......................$2.40
Colors: Gloss Green, Gloss Blue,
Gloss Rose, Yellow, Mahogany,
Black, Blue and White, Green and
White, Brown and White, Brown
and Yellow

No. F-32 Basket Girl, 8" high
Per doz......................$12.00
Colors: Seacrest Green, Pink,
Stardew Blue, Yellow, White.

No. LN Jug
½-pt. per doz...............$3.60
1-pt. per doz...............4.80
1-qt. per doz...............8.40
Colors: Same as No. J-1

No. J-6 Pitcher Jug
4 oz. per doz...............$3.00
16 oz. per doz...............4.80
Colors: same as No. J-1

No. J-2 Jug
2 oz. per doz...............$2.40
8 oz. per doz...............2.70
16 oz. per doz...............3.00
Colors: Same as No. J-1

No. F-29 Horse, 5¼" long
Per doz......................$3.60
Colors: Seacrest Green, Stardew
Blue, Yellow, White. All with Black
eyes, mouth and nostrils.

No. RJ Jug, 8 oz.
Per doz......................$2.70
Colors: Same as No. J-1

No. P-1 Ram, 4½" high.
Per doz......................$4.80
Colors: White, Pink, Yellow,
Seacrest Green, Stardew Blue.

No. P-2 Pony, 5¼" long
Per doz......................$4.00
Colors: Same as No. P-1

No. P-3 Burro, 4½" high
Per doz......................$3.60
Colors: Same as No. P-1

THE ZANESVILLE STONEWARE COMPANY
ZANESVILLE, OHIO

Catalog #12 supplement.

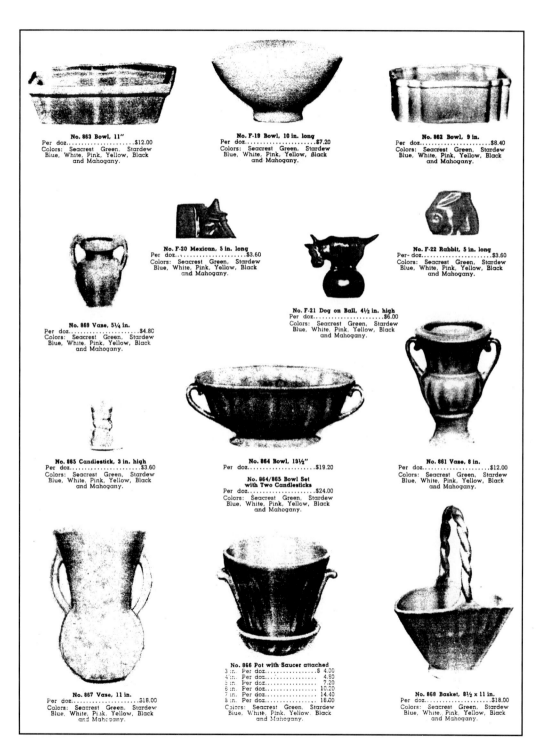

No. 863 Bowl, 11"
Per doz.....................$12.00
Colors: Seacrest Green, Stardew
Blue, White, Pink, Yellow, Black
and Mahogany.

No. F-19 Bowl, 10 in. long
Per doz.....................$7.20
Colors: Seacrest Green, Stardew
Blue, White, Pink, Yellow, Black
and Mahogany.

No. 862 Bowl, 9 in.
Per doz.....................$8.40
Colors: Seacrest Green, Stardew
Blue, White, Pink, Yellow, Black
and Mahogany.

No. F-20 Mexican, 5 in. long
Per doz.....................$3.60
Colors: Seacrest Green, Stardew
Blue, White, Pink, Yellow, Black
and Mahogany.

No. F-22 Rabbit, 5 in. long
Per doz.....................$3.60
Colors: Seacrest Green, Stardew
Blue, White, Pink, Yellow, Black
and Mahogany.

No. 869 Vase, 5¼ in.
Per doz.....................$4.80
Colors: Seacrest Green, Stardew
Blue, White, Pink, Yellow, Black
and Mahogany.

No. F-21 Dog on Ball, 4½ in. high
Per doz.....................$6.00
Colors: Seacrest Green, Stardew
Blue, White, Pink, Yellow, Black
and Mahogany.

No. 865 Candlestick, 3 in. high
Per doz.....................$3.60
Colors: Seacrest Green, Stardew
Blue, White, Pink, Yellow, Black
and Mahogany.

No. 864 Bowl, 13½"
Per doz.....................$19.20

No. 864/865 Bowl Set
with Two Candlesticks
Per doz.....................$24.00
Colors: Seacrest Green, Stardew
Blue, White, Pink, Yellow, Black
and Mahogany.

No. 861 Vase, 6 in.
Per doz.....................$12.00
Colors: Seacrest Green, Stardew
Blue, White, Pink, Yellow, Black
and Mahogany.

No. 867 Vase, 11 in.
Per doz.....................$18.00
Colors: Seacrest Green, Stardew
Blue, White, Pink, Yellow, Black
and Mahogany.

No. 866 Pot with Saucer attached
3 in. Per doz.............$ 4.00
4 in. Per doz............. 4.80
5 in. Per doz............. 7.20
6 in. Per doz............. 10.20
7 in. Per doz............. 14.40
8 in. Per doz............. 18.00
Colors: Seacrest Green, Stardew
Blue, White, Pink, Yellow, Black
and Mahogany.

No. 868 Basket, 8½ x 11 in.
Per doz.....................$18.00
Colors: Seacrest Green, Stardew
Blue, White, Pink, Yellow, Black
and Mahogany.

Catalog #12 supplement.

No. BA-16 Bowl, 6"
Per doz.................$6.00
Colors: Seacrest Green, Stardew
Blue, Gloss Green, Gloss Blue,
White, Pink, Yellow, Black.

No. BA-5 Jardiniere, 4"
Per doz.....................$2.40
Colors: Seacrest Green, Stardew Blue,
Gloss Green, Gloss Blue, White,
Gloss Rose, Pink, Yellow, Black

No. BA-17 Bowl, 5"
Per doz.................$2.40
Colors: Seacrest Green, Stardew
Blue, White, Yellow, Black,
Gloss Rose, Mahogany.

No. RG-1 Pot, 7¼" x 7¼"
Per doz.....................$6.00
Colors: Seacrest Green, Stardew
Blue, White, Yellow, Black. The
top edge of the pot is unglazed

No. 341 Vase, 4½"
Per doz.................$3.60
Colors: Seacrest Green Stardew
Blue, White, Yellow, Pink, Black.

No. 342 Vase, 7"
Per doz.....................$6.00
Colors: Gloss Green, Gloss Blue,
White, Black, Gloss Rose, Yellow.

No. 337 Vase, 10"
Per doz.....................$12.00
Colors: Seacrest Green, Gloss Blue,
White, Burgundy.

No. 338 Vase, 10"
Per doz.....................$14.40
Colors: Seacrest Green, Stardew
Blue, Pink, Yellow, White, Black.

No. 336 Vase, 8" high x 9½" wide
Per doz.....................$12.00
Colors: Seacrest Green, Stardew
Blue, White, Yellow, Black, Pink,
Gloss Green, Gloss Blue, Gloss Rose.

No. 339 Bowl, 13"
Per doz.....................$19.20
Colors: Seacrest Green, Gloss Blue,
Stardew Blue, Yellow, White, Pink,
Black.

No. 230 Vase
12" per doz.....................$15.00
15" per doz.....................24.00
18" per doz.....................36.00
Colors: Apple Green, Seacrest Green
Gloss Blue, White, Yellow, Gloss
Rose, Black.

No. 320 Jardiniere
8" per doz.................$ 7.20
9" per doz.................10.80
10" per doz.................14.40
12" per doz.................24.00
Colors: Seacrest Green, Stardew
Blue, White, Yellow, Black. The 12"
size is designed to hold a 10"
Standard Pot; the smaller sizes are
to take transfers from or to hold
¾ Pots.

No. 340 Bowl, 12½"
Per doz.....................$12.00
Colors: Seacrest Green, Gloss Blue,
Stardew Blue, White, Pink, Gloss
Rose, Black, Yellow.

Catalog #12 supplement.

No. F-26 Pup, 7½" long
Per doz......................$6.00
Colors: All White, with Blue collar, Red tongue, and Black eyes and nose.

No. F-25 Cat, 6½" long
Per doz......................$3.60
Colors: Seacrest Green, Stardew Blue, Yellow, White. All with Black eyes, mouth, and whiskers.

No. F-30 Baby Shoe, 4" long
Per doz......................$2.40
Colors: Stardew Blue, Pink, Seacrest Green, White, Yellow.

No. F-28 Boy at Well, 4" hi
Per doz......................
Colors: Seacrest Green, Sta Blue, Yellow, White, Pink

No. F-29 Horse, 5¼" long
Per doz......................$3.60
Colors: Seacrest Green, Stardew Blue, Yellow, White. All with Black eyes, mouth and nostrils.

No. F-24 Dutch Shoe, 7½" long
Per doz......................$3.60
Colors: Seacrest Green, Stardew Blue, Yellow, White, Pink, Black.

No. F-23 Dutch Girl, 8½" high
Per doz......................$12.00
Colors: All White with cap, apron, and shoes trimmed in Red, Blue Yellow, and Green.

No. F-27 Dog and Hamper, 4¼"
Per doz......................
Colors: Seacrest Green, Sta Blue, Yellow, White. All Red eyes and nose.

No. F-22 Rabbit, 5 in. long
Per doz......................$3.60
Colors: Seacrest Green, Stardew Blue, White, Pink, Yellow, Black and Mahogany.

No. F-31 Bear, 6" long
Per doz......................$3.60
Colors: White, Black, Brown, Yellow, Seacrest Green, Gloss Blue.

No. F-20 Mexican, 5 in. long
Per doz......................$3.60
Colors: Seacrest Green, Stardew Blue, White, Pink, Yellow, Black and Mahogany.

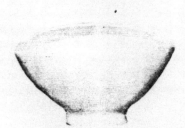

No. F-19 Bowl, 10 in. long
Per doz......................$7.20
Seacrest Green, Stardew Blue, White, Pink, Yellow, Black and Mahogany.

No. RG-2 Pot
Seacrest Green, Stardew Blue, White, Yellow, Black. The top edge of the pot is unglazed.
6" per doz...................$ 6.00
7" per doz................... 8.40
8" per doz................... 10.80

No. 100X Bird Bath
15 in. dia. x 17 in. high
Seacrest Green, Stardew B White, Gloss Green, Yellow, Blue, Pink, Gloss Rose.
Per doz. ....

Catalog #13 novelties.

The
Zanesville Stoneware Company
Zanesville, Ohio, U. S. A.

Catalogue No. 14R

Manufacturers of

Art Ware and Garden Ware

No. 847 Jar
16½" tall opening 5½". Each $8.00

THE QUALITY of the ware illustrated on these pages has been tested by time and use. A hard-fired body and a variety of colored glazes are joined to add strength, durability and dependability to pleasing appearance.

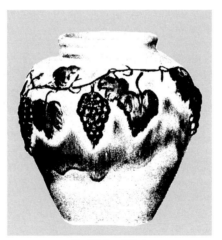

No. 849 Jar, 16½ in.
Gray with Blue Grapes and Russet
with Burgundy Grapes.
Each $20.00

No. 106 Jar
15" tall, opening 5", Each....$ 6.00
18" tall, opening 6", Each.... 9.00
22" tall, opening 8", Each.... 13.00

COLORS are Seacrest Green, Gloss Green, Gloss Blue, Royal Gloss Blue, Gloss Rose, Gloss Yellow, Black, White and a few two-tone shadings or over-flows at ten per cent extra. Unless it is otherwise specified, items are available in all plain colors.

PRICES are F. O. B. Zanesville, Ohio.

Catalog #14R, 1951.

No. 869 Vase, 5¼ in.
Per doz. $8.00
Seacrest Green, Gloss Blue,
White, Yellow.

No. 858 Vase, 6 in.
Gloss Green, Gloss Blue, White,
Yellow, Seacrest Green.
Per doz. $9.00

No. 342 Vase, 7 in.
Per doz. $9.00
Gloss Green, Gloss Blue, White,
Yellow.

No. 792 Vase, 6 in.
Seacrest Green, Gloss Blue, White,
Yellow. Per doz. $8.00
8 in.
Per doz. $12.00
Seacrest Green, Gloss Blue, White.

No. 330 Vase
Gloss Green, Seacrest Green, Gloss
Blue, White, Yellow.
6 in. Per doz.............$ 6.00
8 in. Per doz.............$ 9.00
10 in. Per doz.............$15.00

No. 861 Vase, 8 in.
Per doz. $18.00
Seacrest Green, Gloss Blue, White,
Yellow.

No. 829 Vase, 8½ in.
Seacrest Green, Yellow, Gloss Blue,
White.
Per doz.................$12.00

No. 837 Vase, 8½ in.
Seacrest Green, Gloss Blue, White.
Per doz.................$12.00

No. 851 Vase, 8x8 in.
Gloss Green, Seacrest Green, Gloss
Blue, White.
Per doz. $18.00
5x6 in.
Seacrest Green, Gloss Blue, Yellow,
White.
Per doz. $8.00

No. 4VH Vase, 12 in.
Gloss Green, Gloss Blue, White,
Yellow, Seacrest Green.
Per doz. $36.00

No. 867 Vase, 11 in.
Per doz..................$30.00
Seacrest Green, Gloss Blue, White,
Yellow.

No. J Vase, 12 in.
Gloss Green, Gloss Blue, White,
Seacrest Green.
Per doz. $24.00

No. 230 Vase
9" per doz..............$12.00
12" per doz.............$24.00
15" per doz.............$40.00
18" per doz.............$64.00
Seacrest Green, Gloss Blue, White,
Yellow.

No. 0 Jardiniere
Seacrest Green, Gloss Green, Gloss
Blue, White, Yellow.
4 in. per doz..............$ 4.80
5 in. per doz..............$ 6.00
6 in. per doz..............$ 7.50
7 in. per doz..............$ 9.60
8 in. per doz..............$14.40
9 in. per doz..............$18.00
10 in. per doz..............$24.00

No. 320 Jardiniere
6" per doz. ....$ 7.20
7" per doz. $10.80
8" per doz. $14.40
9" per doz. $18.00
10" per doz. $23.40
12" per doz. $36.00
Seacrest Green, Gloss Blue, White,
Yellow. The 12" size is designed to
hold a 10" Standard Pot; the
smaller sizes are to take transfers
from or to hold ¾ Pots.

No. 333 Jardiniere
Seacrest Green, Gloss Blue, Yellow,
Gloss Green, White.
5" per doz. ....$ 7.50
6" per doz. $10.80
7" per doz. $16.20
8" per doz. $24.00

Catalog #14R, 1951.

257

No. F-1 Bowl, 4" high
Seacrest Green, Gloss Blue, Yellow,
White.
Per doz. $6.00

No. F-2 Bowl, 4" high
Same as F-1.

No. F-3 Bowl, 4" high
Colors and prices same as No F-1.

No. BA-1 Bowl
Seacrest Green, Gloss Green, Gloss
Blue, Yellow, White.
6 in per doz. ....$ 9.00
8 in. per doz. $18.00

No. BA-15 Bowl, 6 in.
Gloss Blue, Seacrest Green, Yellow,
White. Per doz. $7.20

No. 311 Window Box.
4¼"x15", depth 4¼"
Seacrest Green, Gloss Green, Gloss
Blue, White, Yellow.
Per doz. $30.00

No. 312 Window Pot
4¼"x5", depth 5¾"
Same colors as No. 311. Per doz.
$9.60. Nos. 311 and 312 may be
arranged in several different combinations to make up Window
Boxes of any length.

No. BA-21 Bowl, 6 in.
Gloss Green, Gloss Blue, White.
Per doz. $9.00

No. 806 Bowl, Rectangular Shape
Seacrest Green, Gloss Blue, Yellow,
White.
6"x10". Per doz. $18.00
8½"x12". Per doz. 37.50
10"x15". Per doz. 75.00
12"x18". Per doz. 120.00

No. 863 Bowl, 11"
Per doz. $16.00
Colors: Seacrest Green, Gloss Blue,
White, Yellow.

No. 805 Bowl, Square Shape
Gloss Green, Gloss Blue, Yellow,
White.
9" x 9". Per doz........$18.00
12½" x 12½". Per doz.... 37.50
16" x 16". Per doz....... 75.00

No. BA-16 Bowl, 6"
Per doz. $9.00
Colors: Seacrest Green, Gloss
Green, Gloss Blue, White, Yellow.

No. 862 Bowl, 9 in.
Per doz. $12.00
Colors: Seacrest Green, Gloss Blue,
White, Yellow.

No. 871 Bowl, 11 in.
Gloss Green, Gloss Blue, White,
Yellow.
Per doz. $16.00

No. 303 Window Box. 12 in.
Seacrest Green, Gloss Green, White,
Gloss Blue, Yellow.
Per doz. $24.00

No. 870 Bowl, 9 in.
Gloss Green, Gloss Blue, White
Yellow.
Per doz. $12.00

**No. 783 Square Pot
with Saucer Attached**
Gloss Green, Seacrest Green, Gloss
Blue, Yellow, White.
4 in. Per doz. $8.00
5 in. Per doz. 12.00
4 in. Pot only. Per doz. 5.40
5 in. Pot only. Per doz...... 8.00

No. 856 Flower Pot
Gloss Green, Seacrest Green, Gloss
Blue, Yellow, White.
5 in. Per doz. ....$ 7.20
6 in. Per doz. 10.80
7 in. Per doz. 14.40
8 in. Per doz. 18.00
9 in. Per doz. 23.40

**No. 850 Flower Pot
with Saucer Attached**
Gloss Green, Seacrest Green, Gloss
Blue, Yellow, White.
3 in. Per doz. ....$ 5.40
4 in. Per doz. 7.20
5 in. Per doz. 9.00
6 in. Per doz. 13.50
7 in. Per doz. 18.00
8 in. Per doz. 23.40

No. 560 Flower Pot and Saucer
Gloss Green, Seacrest Green, Gloss
Blue, Yellow, White
5 in. Per doz. ....$ 9.00
6 in. Per doz. 13.50
7 in. Per doz. 18.00
8 in. Per doz. 23.40
9 in. Per doz. 29.25
10 in. Per doz. 36.00
11 in. Per doz. 43.20
12 in. Per doz. 54.00

Catalog #14R, 1951.

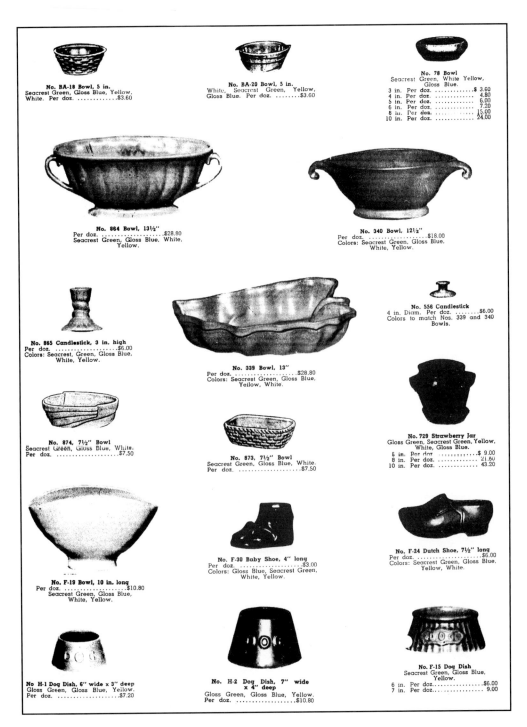

No. BA-18 Bowl, 5 in.
Seacrest Green, Gloss Blue, Yellow,
White. Per doz. $3.60

No. BA-20 Bowl, 5 in.
White, Seacrest Green, Yellow,
Gloss Blue. Per doz. $3.60

No. 78 Bowl
Seacrest Green, White Yellow,
Gloss Blue.
3 in. Per doz. ....$ 3.60
4 in. Per doz. 4.80
5 in. Per doz. 6.00
6 in. Per doz. 7.20
8 in. Per doz. 15.00
10 in. Per doz. 24.00

No. 864 Bowl, 13½"
Per doz. $28.80
Seacrest Green, Gloss Blue, White,
Yellow.

No. 340 Bowl, 12½"
Per doz. $18.00
Colors: Seacrest Green, Gloss Blue,
White, Yellow.

No. 865 Candlestick, 3 in. high
Per doz. $6.00
Colors: Seacrest, Green, Gloss Blue,
White, Yellow.

No. 339 Bowl, 13"
Per doz. $28.80
Colors: Seacrest Green, Gloss Blue,
Yellow, White.

No. 556 Candlestick
4 in. Diam. Per doz. $6.00
Colors to match Nos. 339 and 340
Bowls.

No. 874, 7½" Bowl
Seacrest Green, Gloss Blue, White.
Per doz. $7.50

No. 873, 7½" Bowl
Seacrest Green, Gloss Blue, White.
Per doz. $7.50

No. 729 Strawberry Jar
Gloss Green, Seacrest Green, Yellow,
White, Gloss Blue.
6 in. Per doz. ....$ 9.00
8 in. Per doz. 21.60
10 in. Per doz. 43.20

No. F-19 Bowl, 10 in. long
Per doz. $10.80
Seacrest Green, Gloss Blue,
White, Yellow.

No. F-30 Baby Shoe, 4" long
Per doz. $3.00
Colors: Gloss Blue, Seacrest Green,
White, Yellow.

No. F-24 Dutch Shoe, 7½" long
Per doz. $6.00
Colors: Seacrest Green, Gloss Blue,
Yellow, White.

No H-1 Dog Dish, 6" wide x 3" deep
Gloss Green, Gloss Blue, Yellow.
Per doz. $7.20

No. H-2 Dog Dish, 7" wide x 4" deep
Gloss Green, Gloss Blue, Yellow.
Per doz. $10.80

No. F-15 Dog Dish
Seacrest Green, Gloss Blue,
Yellow.
6 in. Per doz. $6.00
7 in. Per doz. 9.00

Catalog #14R, 1951.

No. 515 Pitcher, 5-pt.
Gloss Green, Gloss Blue, Gloss
Rose, Yellow.
Per doz. $24.00

No. 515X Mug 16 oz.
Colors to match No. 515
Per doz. $6.00

No. D-10 Bowl 6"
Gloss Green, Gloss Blue, Mahog-
any, and Yellow.
Per doz. $6.00

No. D-12 Pitcher 24 oz.
Colors to match No. D-10
Per doz. $9.00

No. 401 Pitcher, 3 in.
Seacrest Green, Gloss Blue, Yellow,
White, Mahogany.
Per doz. $3.60

No. 402 Sugar Bowl, 2½" high
Colors to match No. 401
Per doz. $3.60

No. 44 Mug
Gloss Green, Gloss Blue, Mahogany, Yellow
10 oz. Per doz. $6.00
12 oz. Per doz. 6.00

No. RB Casserole
Gloss Green, Gloss Blue, Mahogany,
Brown and Yellow.
6 oz. Per doz. $4.80
12 oz. Per doz. 6.00
16 oz. Per doz. 8.40

No. F-7 Cigarette Box, 4¼"
Seacrest Green, Gloss Blue, Yellow,
Black, White, Gloss Rose.
Per doz. $12.00

No. D-18 Nut Dish 2-¾ in.
Seacrest Green, Gloss Rose, Yellow,
Gloss Blue, White, Black.
Per doz. $1.80

No. F-10 Ash Tray, 4 in.
Seacrest Green, Gloss Blue, White,
Black, Yellow, Gloss Rose.
Per doz. $3.00

No. RP Plate 7 in.
Gloss Green, Gloss Blue, Mahog-
any, and Yellow.
Per doz. $4.80

**Nos. J-1, J-3, J-4, J-5, J-9, J-10, and
J-13 Jugs, 2 oz.**
Per doz. $3.60
Gloss Green, Gloss Blue, Gloss,
Rose, Yellow, Mahogany, Black,
Blue and White, Green and White,
Brown and White, Brown and
Yellow

No. LN Jug
½-pt. per doz. ....$ 6.00
1-pt. per doz. 9.60
1-qt. per doz. 14.40

No. J-6 Pitcher Jug
4 oz. per doz. $4.50
8 oz. per doz. 6.00
16 oz per doz. 9.60

No. J-2 Jug
2 oz. per doz. $3.60
8 oz. per doz. 4.50
16 oz. per doz. 7.50
Colors: Same as No. J-1

No. RJ Jug, 8 oz.
Per doz. $4.50
Colors: Same as No. J-1

Catalog #14R, 1951.

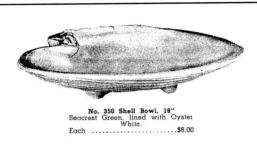

No. 350 Shell Bowl, 18"
Seacrest Green, lined with Oyster
White.
Each $8.00

No. F-12 Hanging Strawberry Pot
with Chain, 5 in.
Seacrest Green, Gloss Blue, Gloss
Rose, White, Yellow
Per doz. $14.40

No. 202 Flared Top Vase
Black, White, Seacrest Green, Gloss
Blue.
3x4½ in. Per doz. $4.20
4x6 in. Per doz. 7.20
3x9 in. Per doz. 9.00
4½x9 in. Per doz. 10.80
4x12 in. Per doz. 12.00
5½x10 in. Per doz. 14.40
4½x15 in. Per doz. 18.00
5½x18 in. Per doz. 30.00

No. 730 Flower Pot,
Standard ¾-Pot Size
Gloss Green, Seacrest Green, Gloss
Blue, Yellow, Black, Gloss Rose,
White.
5 in. Per doz. ....$ 7.20
6 in. Per doz. 10.80
7 in. Per doz. 14.40
8 in. Per doz. 18.00
9 in. Per doz. 23.40
10 in. Per doz. 28.80

No. 601 Bulb Pan
Seacrest Green, White, Gloss Blue,
Yellow, Gloss Rose.
9" per doz. $23.40
10" per doz. 28.80
12" per doz. 43.20

No. 868 Basket, 8½x11 in.
Per doz. $24.00
Colors: Seacrest Green, Gloss Blue,
White, Yellow.

No. 825 Jar
With Iron Stand, 22" high overall.
Each $20.50 22.00
Jar only, 16½" tall, opening 8".
Each $11.00
Iron Stand Only. Each.......$ 9.00 11.00

No. 729 Strawberry Jar
12 in. Each.................$ 9.00
16 in. Each................. 18.00
21 in. Each................. 36.00

These larger jars, No. 729, No. 825,
and No. 790, are available in all
plain colors; and No. 825 and No.
790 in a few very pleasing over-
flows at ten per cent above the
listed prices.

No. 790 Jar
17" tall, opening 7". Each...$11.00
With Iron Stand, 23" high overall
Each $20.50 22.0

Catalog #14R, 1951.

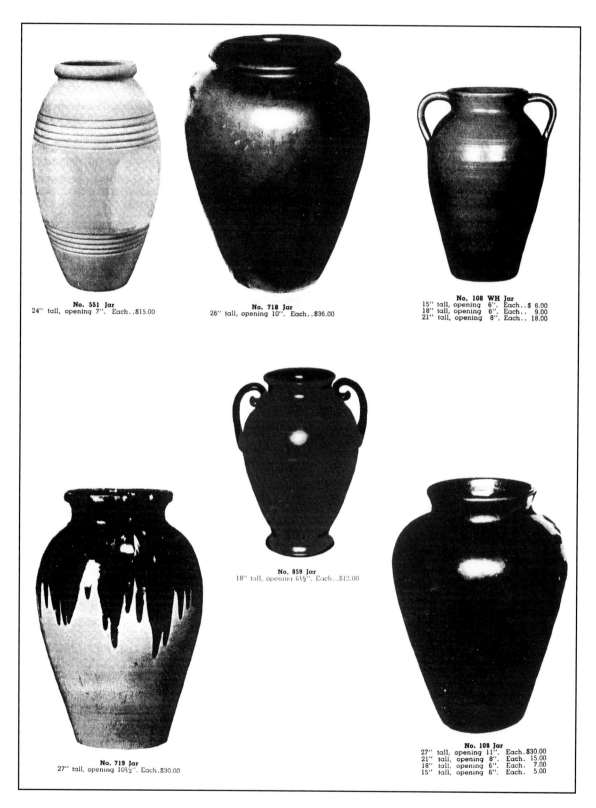

No. 551 Jar
24″ tall, opening 7″. Each..$15.00

No. 718 Jar
26″ tall, opening 10″. Each..$36.00

No. 108 WH Jar
15″ tall, opening 6″. Each..$ 6.00
18″ tall, opening 6″. Each.. 9.00
21″ tall, opening 8″. Each.. 18.00

No. 859 Jar
18″ tall, opening 6½″. Each..$12.00

No. 719 Jar
27″ tall, opening 10½″. Each..$30.00

No. 108 Jar
27″ tall, opening 11″. Each.$30.00
21″ tall, opening 8″. Each. 15.00
18″ tall, opening 6″. Each. 7.00
15″ tall, opening 6″. Each. 5.00

Catalog #14R, 1951.

No. 1 Umbrella or Sand Jar
10 x 21 in.
Per doz. $72.00

No. 2 Umbrella or Sand Jar
10 x 21 in.
Per doz. $72.00

No. 4 Umbrella or Sand Jar
11 x 21 in.
Per doz. $90.00

No. 100X Bird Bath
15 in. dia. x 17 in. high
Each $6.50

No. 540 Villa Pot
16″ Top diameter. Each...... $8.00
22″ Top diameter. Each...... 24.00

No. 538 Bird Bath
26″ tall by 19″ diameter
Stone finish, green trim, each $10.00
Glazed colors, each 15.00

No. 550 Jar, 16″ tall
Each $8.00

No. 553 Porch Pot, 13″ top diameter
Each $4.00

No. 717 Jar, 20 in.
Each $16.00

No. 558 Jar, 15″ tall, opening 10″
Each $8.00

No. 585 Urn, 14″ top diameter
Each $7.00

Catalog #14R, 1951.

263

The Zanesville Stoneware Co.
ZANESVILLE, OHIO

NO. 825—Jar with Iron Stand

Jar, 16½" high; diam. of opening, 8"
Jar with Stand, 22" high over all.
Jar Only............................$ 7.00 each
Jar with Iron Stand......$10.00 each
F. O. B. Zanesville, Ohio
Colors:—Matt Green, Royal Blue, Gloss
Green, Gloss Blue, Gloss Rose, Gloss Yel-
low, Gloss Black, Neptune (Green with
rust-colored markings), Green flow over
Gray, Blue flow over Gray, Black flow
over Green.

Catalog #14R, 1951.

The Zanesville Stoneware Co.
ZANESVILLE, OHIO

NO. 538—Glazed Bird Bath

20" diam., 24" high

Each $5.00

F. O. B. Zanesville, Ohio

Colors:—Gloss Green, Gloss Blue, Gloss Rose
and Matt Green

HANGING BASKET

10 in. Diameter
$24.00 Per Doz.
Chains included

A beautiful basket for direct planting of vines etc., for shading and
shielding the porch.

264

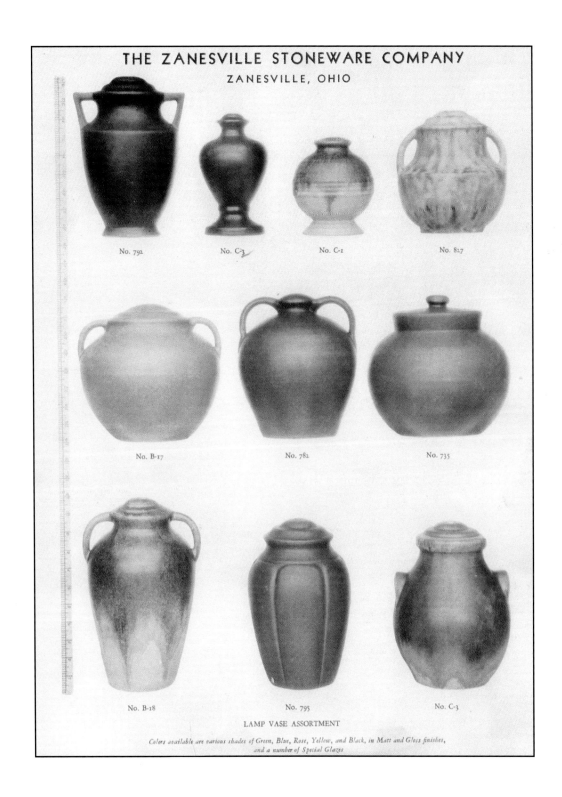

THE ZANESVILLE STONEWARE COMPANY
ZANESVILLE, OHIO

No. 792   No. C-3   No. C-1   No. 827

No. B-17   No. 782   No. 735

No. B-18   No. 795   No. C-3

LAMP VASE ASSORTMENT

*Colors available are various shades of Green, Blue, Rose, Yellow, and Black, in Matt and Gloss finishes,
and a number of Special Glazes*

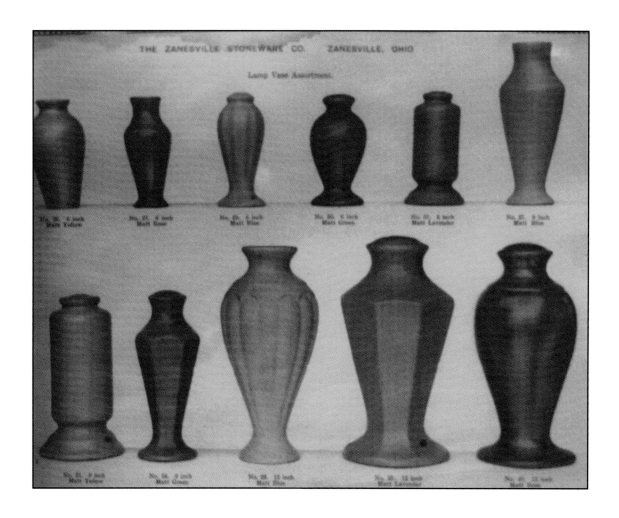

1960s Stoneage Modern catalog.

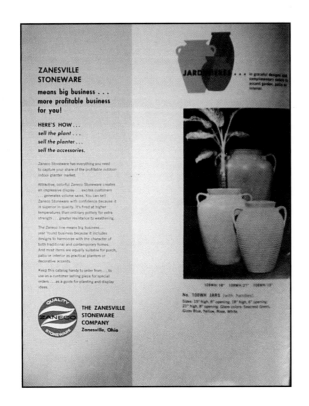

1960s Stoneage Modern catalog.

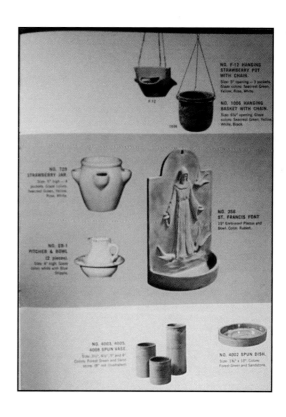

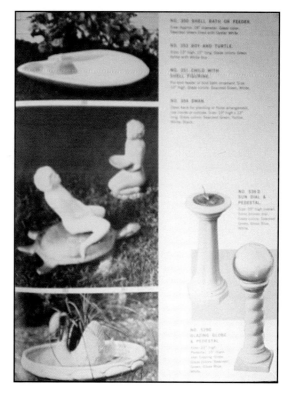

1960s Stoneage Modern catalog.

Bibliography

Birks, Tony. *The Complete Pottery Companion.* Bullfinch Press. Little, Brown and Company, Inc., Canada.

Garden Ware Special April Issue, *Crockery and Glass Journal*, 1930 and 1931.

A Guide to Pottery. Zanesville Chamber of Commerce, 1999.

The Journal of the American Art Pottery Association, November – December 1997.

Lehner, Lois. *Lehner's Encyclopedia of U.S. Marks on Pottery, Porcelain, and Clay.* Collector Books, Paducah, Kentucky, 1988.

Milman Linn Progressive Potter, American Ceramics Society, September 15, 1943.

Ralston, Pat. Notes from trip to Zanesville, October 1989.

Schneider, Norris. "The Zanesville Stoneware Company is oldest pottery in city," *Zanesville Times-Signal*, September 8, 1957.

Schneider, Norris. "31 potteries operated in city during the late 19th century," *Zanesville Times-Signal*, November 24, 1957.

Sims, Michael. *Ohio Encaustic Tile Company Flash Point*, Vol. 5, No. 2.

Slavitt, Robert. *Francis F. Duggan the Potter 1926.* Westelm Publications, Norwalk, Connecticut, 1996.

Tartar, Jabe. "The Art of Clewell Pottery." *The Antiques Journal*, February 1970. Antiques Publications, Emmitsburg, Maryland.

Vilain, Jean Francois, and Roger S. Wieck. *Zanesville Stoneware.* Published by the Journal of the American Art Pottery Association, March 1986.

Zanesville City Directory, 1892, 1893.

Zanesville Daily Courier, June 28, 1883; May 22, 1884; September 8, 1894; February 2, 1886; December 22, 1886; January 19, 1887; January 22, 1887; August 24, 1887.

Zanesville Signal, February 10, 1921.

"The Zanesville Stoneware Marks 100th Year." *Zanesville Times Recorder*, January 22, 1989.

Zanesville Times Recorder, February 26, 1940.

Verses from "Rubaiyat of Omar Khayyam" rendered into English verse by Edward Fitzgerald. Illustration of the Master Potter by French illustrator Edmund DuLac.

About the Authors

Jon Rans, native Hoosier, artist, musician, author, and conservator/restorer, has many published articles on various American Art potteries and related subjects and is author along with Mark Eckelman of the *1999 Collectors Encyclopedia of Muncie Pottery*. He has worked as a professional photographer and enjoys collecting and researching little-known Arts and Crafts potteries. The first piece of pottery that began his interest in ceramics, purchased in 1973, was a beautiful matte green unmarked Zanesville Stoneware piece. Ceramics restoration is his field of expertise, and he has been a conservator/restorer since 1994 and is currently head of the Art Pottery Restoration Department of the New Orleans Conservation Guild. His art studio is maintained in the Faubourg Marigny section of the Old French Quarter of New Orleans where he lives with his wife, Rita.

Glenn Ralston began collecting Zanesville Stoneware in 1976 because of the pleasing color tones and the comfortable, masculine heft. This interest became a "two-fer" while searching flea markets in the Northeast for "ancient" motion picture incidentals for the then-to-be American Museum of the Moving Image. If one sought-after piece wasn't found, the other often could be. Those obsessive acquisitions did prove beneficial, and the rest is history. Born and raised in the Midwest, he has spent most of his professional life in New York City.

Like most others fascinated with the characteristic qualities of Zanesville Stoneware, his inquiries usually led around about to Frank Duggan at the old Norwalk Pot Shop. We are all now indebted to Jon Rans for following the clues and all his hard work in giving new context to an old and interesting story.

Nate Russell has a background in the fine arts, having studied sculpture, photography, and painting at the Rhode Island School of Design. He has worked professionally as art gallery curator, retail store and furniture showroom display artist, ornamental metalworker, and woodworker. He has been dealing in and collecting American vintage ceramics since 1990. He has been a contributor to numerous book projects in the field of collectible ceramics, with a focus on Ohio area mid-line production. In the past several years, he has become deeply involved in researching New England area Arts and Crafts era pottery and tile. He currently lives and maintains a private gallery in the Boston area with his wife Elizabeth and their two young sons, Zane and Luke.